Print Acquisitions 1974–1984

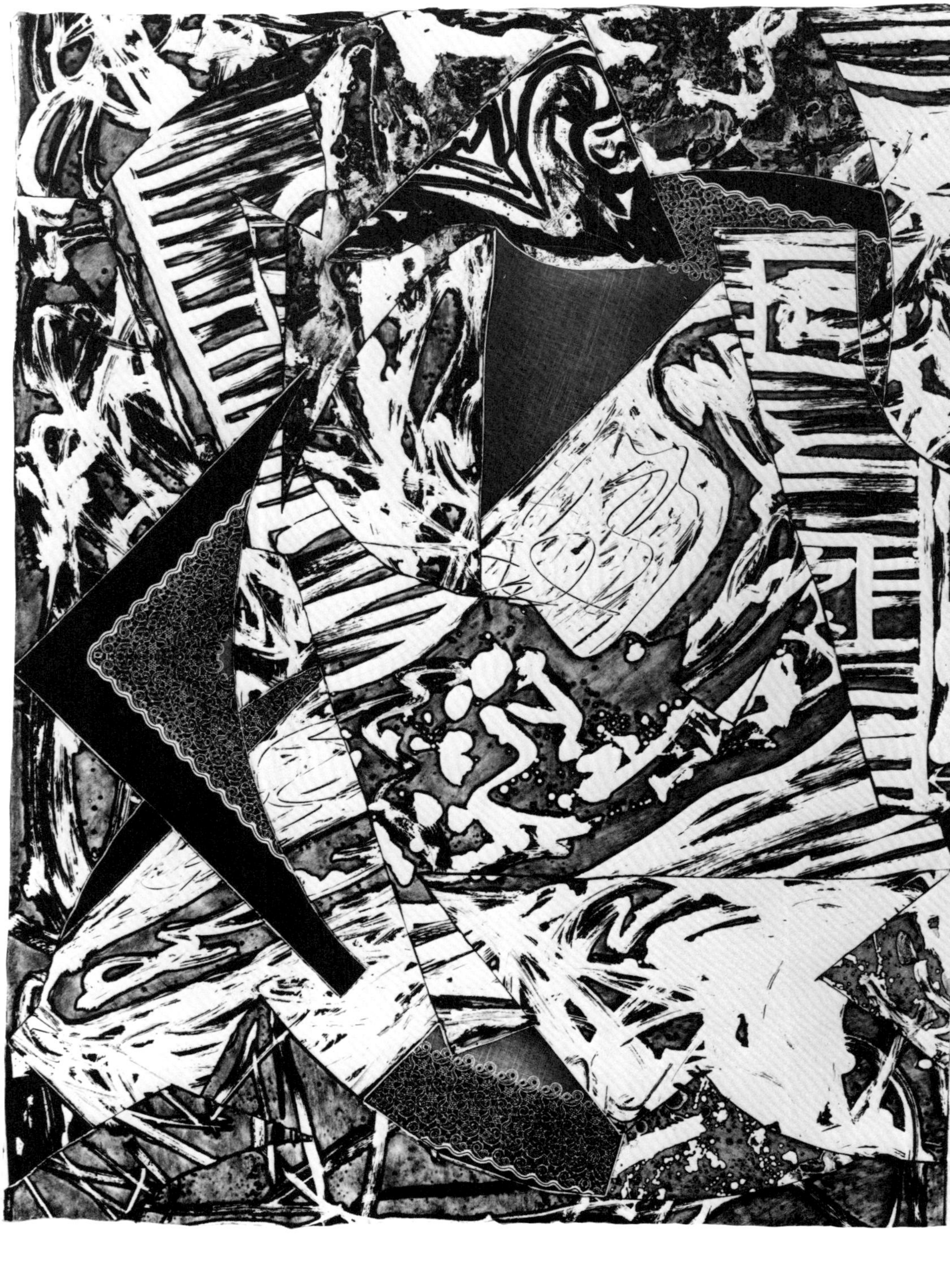

Print Acquisitions 1974–1984

Judith Goldman

Whitney Museum of American Art, New York

Dates of the exhibition: August 29–November 25, 1984

945 Madison Avenue
New York, New York 10021

"Print Acquisitions 1974–1984" is sponsored by the Equitable Life Assurance Society of the United States

This publication was organized at the Whitney Museum of American Art by Doris Palca, Head, Publications and Sales; Sheila Schwartz, Editor; Elaine Koss, Associate Editor; Amy Curtis, Secretary/Assistant; Deborah Leveton, Catalogue Research.

Designer: Katy Homans, Homans|Salsgiver
Typesetter: Michael and Winifred Bixler
Printer: Eastern Press, Inc.

Library of Congress Cataloging in Publication Data

Whitney Museum of American Art.
Print Acquisitions, 1974–1984.

Exhibition, Aug. 29–Nov. 25, 1984
1. Prints, American—Exhibitions. 2. Prints—20th century—United States—Exhibitions. 3. Whitney Museum of American Art—Exhibitions. I. Goldman, Judith. II. Title.
NE508.5.W48 1984 769.973'074'01471 84-15229
ISBN 0-87427-001-4

COVER:
John Storrs, *The Spirit of the Night*, c. 1917.

FRONTISPIECE:
Frank Stella, *Swan Engraving III*, 1982.

PHOTOGRAPH CREDITS:

All photographs are by Geoffrey Clements, with the exception of Frank Stella, *Swan Engraving III*, by Ken Cohen, and Stella, *Talladega Five I* and *Talladega Three I*, by Steven Sloman.

Sponsor's Letter

The Equitable Life Assurance Society of the United States is very pleased to be supporting the activities of the Whitney Museum of American Art once again by sponsoring the exhibition "Print Acquisitions 1974–1984." We are proud to have the opportunity of assisting the Whitney Museum to celebrate an outstanding acquisition program.

This catalogue documents for the first time all print acquisitions since 1974. It will provide a valuable tool for scholars and the general public by making the Permanent Collection more accessible. We commend Judith Goldman, Advisor on Prints, who has determined acquisition priorities, and the members of the Print Committee, who have loyally supported the programs of the Museum and enthusiastically secured the funds for many of these major works.

JOHN B. CARTER
President and Chief Executive Officer
Equitable Life Assurance Society of the United States

Foreword

The Whitney Museum of American Art has acquired an extraordinary group of prints during the past ten years, dating from early in the twentieth century to the present and encompassing a broad range of styles and themes. These acquisitions signal the Museum's commitment to collecting prints that complement works by artists already represented in the Permanent Collection; equally important is the Museum's commitment to adding depth and quality to what is already a comprehensive collection which we hope will be recognized and enjoyed for its unique strengths.

New techniques developed in fine arts printing since 1960 have dramatically expanded the opportunities for aesthetic expression so that more and more contemporary American artists have begun to view their prints as significant aspects of their art. The scope of this exhibition recognizes the importance and quality of printmaking today. We hope that this publication, a complete checklist of prints acquired since the 1974 publication of the catalogue of the collection, will be an important reference work for scholars and the public.

In 1983 the Museum established a Print Committee, whose members come from all over the country to assist in strengthening this important aspect of the Permanent Collection. This exhibition is a testimony to their knowledge, their vision, and their generosity, as well as to the support of other donors who have helped the Whitney Museum to build an important collection of American prints of our century.

TOM ARMSTRONG
Director

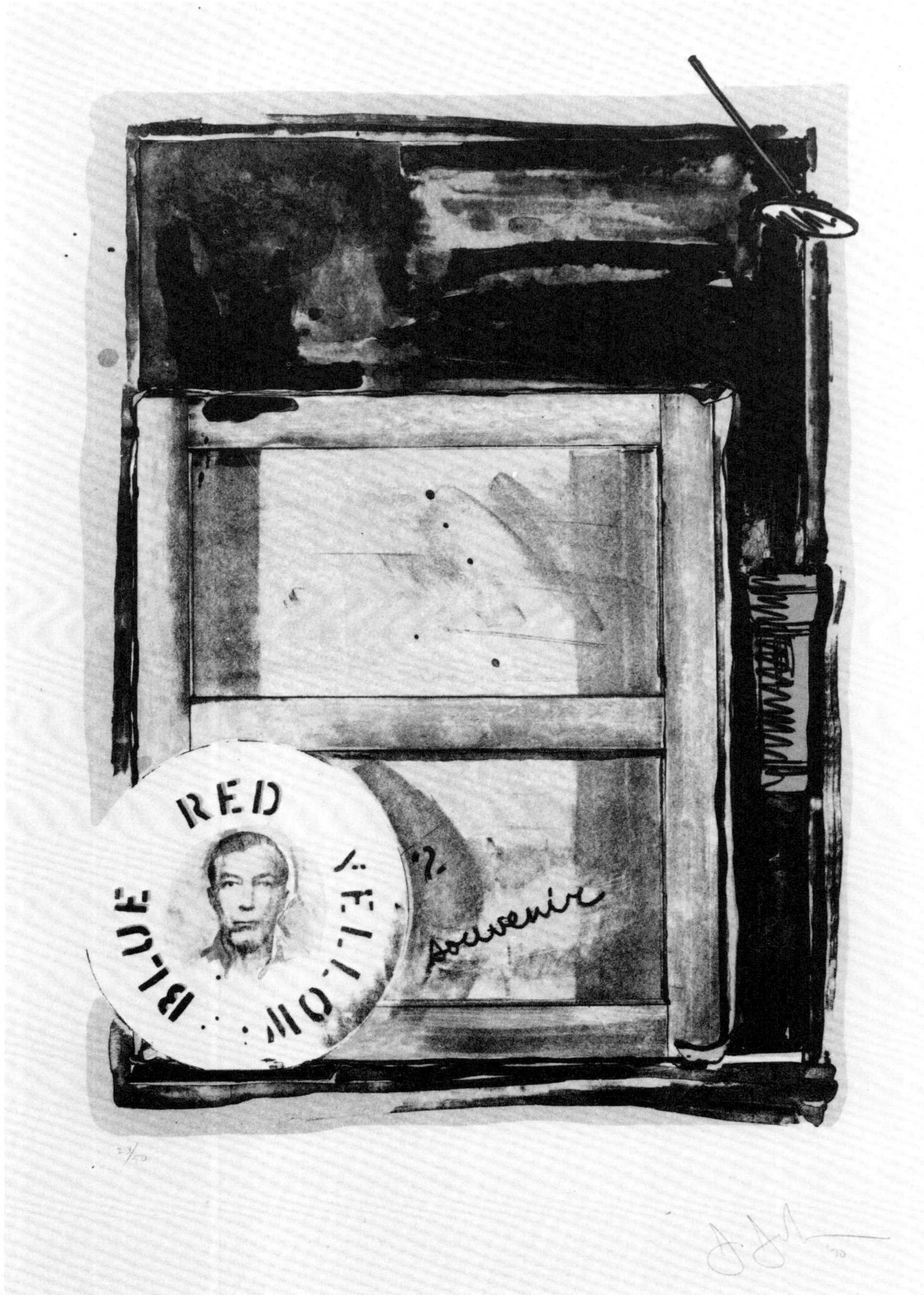

Jasper Johns, *Souvenir*, 1970.

Print Acquisitions 1974–1984

Since 1974, the Whitney Museum of American Art has acquired 513 prints, including 11 portfolios and 6 illustrated books by 149 artists. John Marin's 1911 *Brooklyn Bridge*, made the year Marin returned from Europe to a new, about-to-be vertical city, is the earliest work among these acquisitions. The most recent prints include seventeen works from the *Circuits* series and *Swan Engravings* that Frank Stella began at Tyler Graphics in 1980, as well as prints completed since 1983—woodcuts by Gregory Amenoff and Louisa Chase, lithographs by Susan Rothenberg and Terry Winters. Viewed as a group, the prints offer a history of American graphic art. They show how the print—once a mainly black-and-white, narrative medium suited to album-size images, to the fast sketch and graphic glimpse that tells stories—has become a medium without restrictions, one in which anything technologically feasible is now possible.

These 513 acquisitions also chart changes in style and subject matter, in graphic conventions and printing technologies, in print publishing and the audience for art. Works by George Bellows, Isabel Bishop, Reginald Marsh, and John Sloan trace the persistent course of realism, which at no point is superseded by abstraction. Its hold over artists continues and recent examples include Fairfield Porter's 1971 *Table*, a painterly still life of domestic disarray, and William Bailey's *Still Life No. 6* (1982), a precise, tonal rendering of jars on a ledge.

The graphic forms abstraction takes are equally diverse. Charles Biederman's two unique proofs for *Study for Color Sculpture Outdoors, New York* (1937) show his concern with the effect of color on form. Linear works by Josef Albers and Lyonel Feininger reflect European influence and Bauhaus training, while what is distinctly American about abstract art can be seen in the gestural, spontaneous lithographs by David Smith and Lee Krasner. Printmaking is a fragmented process. Once an image is drawn on wood, stone, or metal, it must be cut or etched, then worked, proofed, and printed. It is not a medium that naturally lends itself to abstraction. Creating a successful abstract print means bending the givens of the medium, and excellent contemporary examples include Helen

Frankenthaler's expansive lithograph *Lot's Wife* (1971); Ellsworth Kelly's spare etching *Wall* (1979); and Frank Stella's classically black-and-white collaged *Swan Engravings* (1982).

In 1957, Tatyana Grosman permanently changed American printmaking when she began publishing prints under the imprint of Universal Limited Art Editions. *Stones*, Mrs. Grosman's first publication, is included here along with other U.L.A.E. issues. Equally important are the publishers that followed the standard Mrs. Grosman set. Prints made after 1960 reflect the taste and predilections of publishers as well as the talents of artists. Richard Artschwager's 1972 *Interior* and Jack Beal's 1974–75 *Self-Portrait* speak for publisher Brooke Alexander's abiding interest in realism and narration. Frank Stella's *Swan Engravings* and *Circuits* prints owe something to Kenneth Tyler's insatiable taste for the technological possibility. And printer-publisher Pat Branstead's extraordinary ability to lay down an aquatint ground is essential to the success of Claes Oldenburg's *Double Screwarch Bridge* series.

A collection serves art, artists, and their public. But since art charts the unknowable and is constantly changing, it is, at best, simplistic to announce collecting goals. With that said, the Whitney Museum of American Art has two major aims in collecting prints: to acquire in depth graphics by artists to whom the Museum has, through exhibitions and acquisitions, made a commitment; and to acquire unique graphic works—trial proofs, state proofs, and monotypes. Important recent acquisitions include groups of prints by Milton Avery, Stuart Davis, Jasper Johns, and Frank Stella; as well as the working and trial proofs for Claes Oldenburg's *Double Screwarch Bridge*, and two of Jasper Johns' monotypes, *Savarin* (1978) and *Untitled* (1983).

Many generous gifts and bequests are reflected in these acquisitions. Especially notable are the fifty prints by Federico Castellon given by Mr. and Mrs. Benjamin Weiss; the seventeen prints from Frank Stella's *Swan Engravings* and *Circuits* series, the promised gift of Judge Steven Robinson; and the bequests of Katherine Schmidt Shubert and Felicia Meyer Marsh. In 1982, the Whitney Museum formed a Print Committee, and its activities are also responsible for the breadth of the collection. I would like to thank the Committee for its generosity and judgment: Chairman Raymond J. Learsy and its members over the last two years—Donald M. Cox, Beth Rudin DeWoody, Mrs. Thomas H. Dittmer, Sidney Kahn, Emily Fisher Landau, Helen Pall, Denise Rich, Mrs. Andrew M. Saul, Richard Shack, Robert Sosnick, Dave H. Williams, and Robert W. Wilson.

JUDITH GOLDMAN

Plates

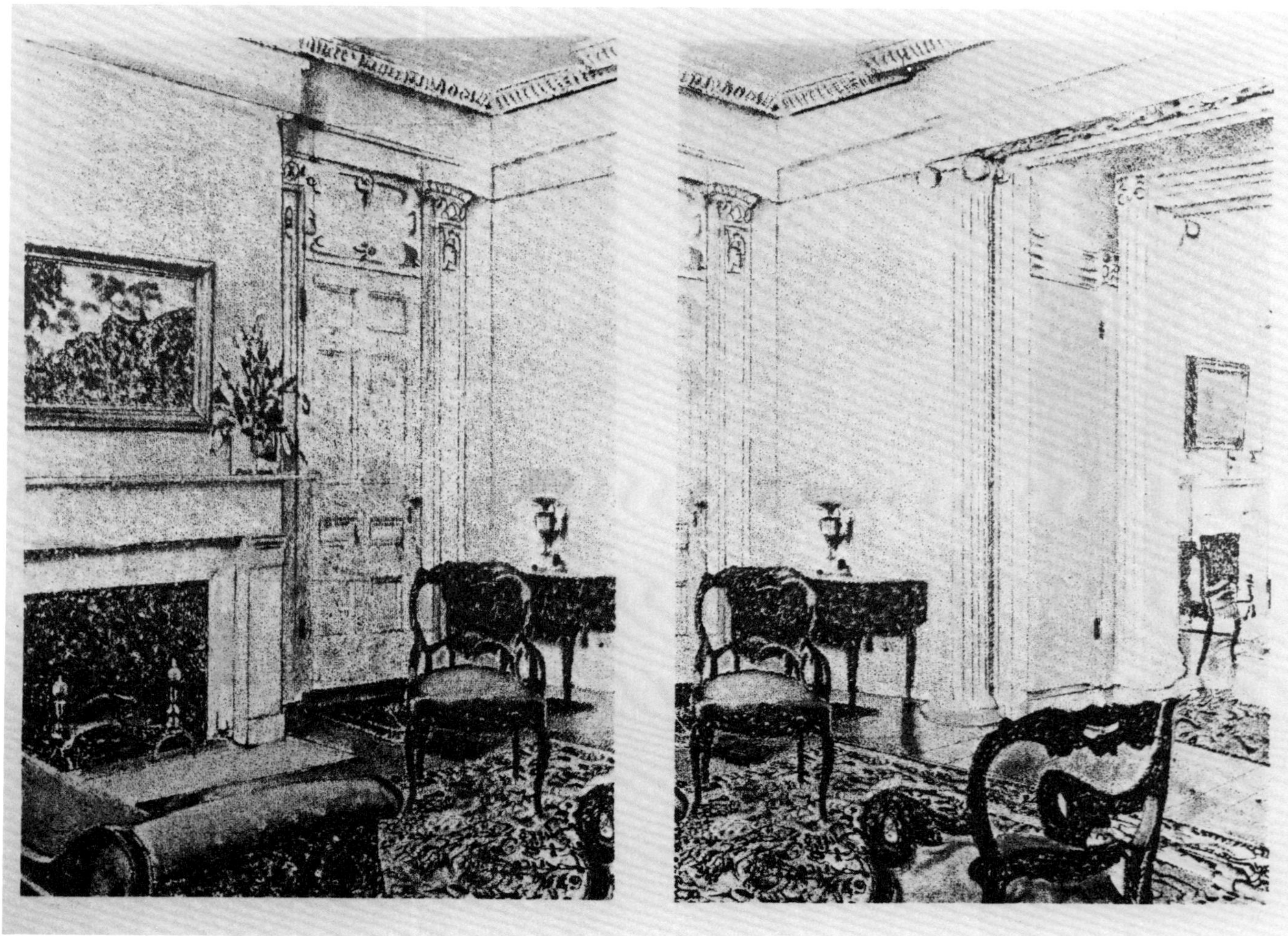

Richard Artschwager, *Interior*, 1972.

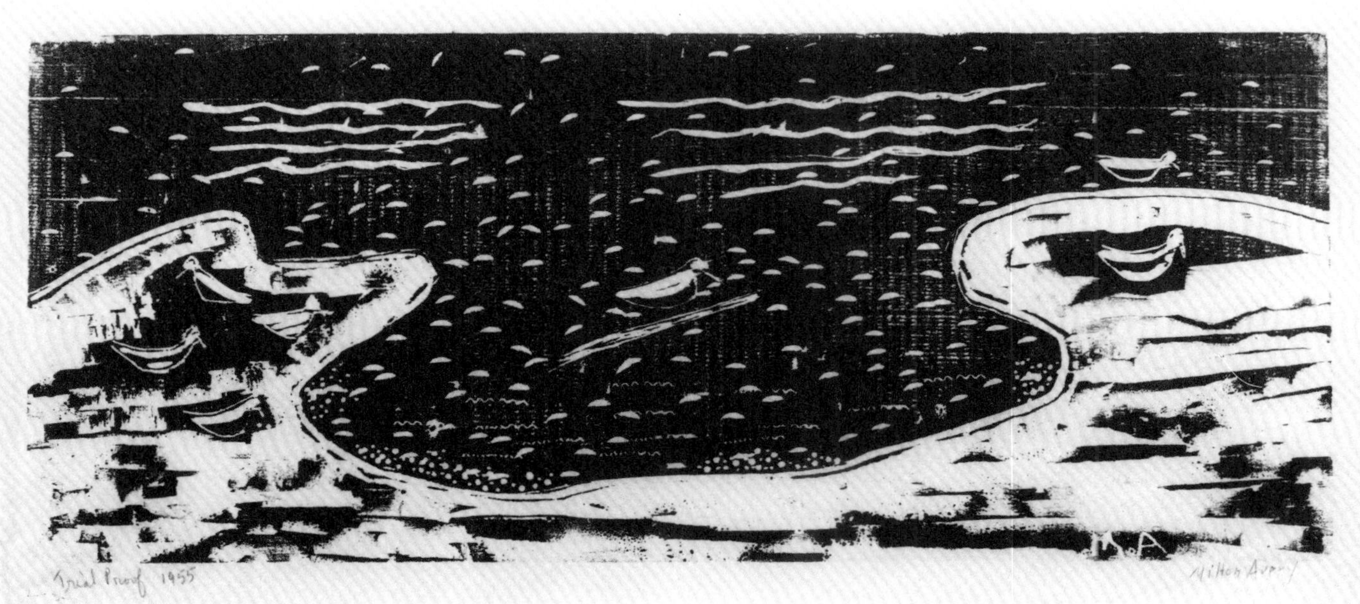

Milton Avery, *Birds and Sea*, Trial Proof, 1955.

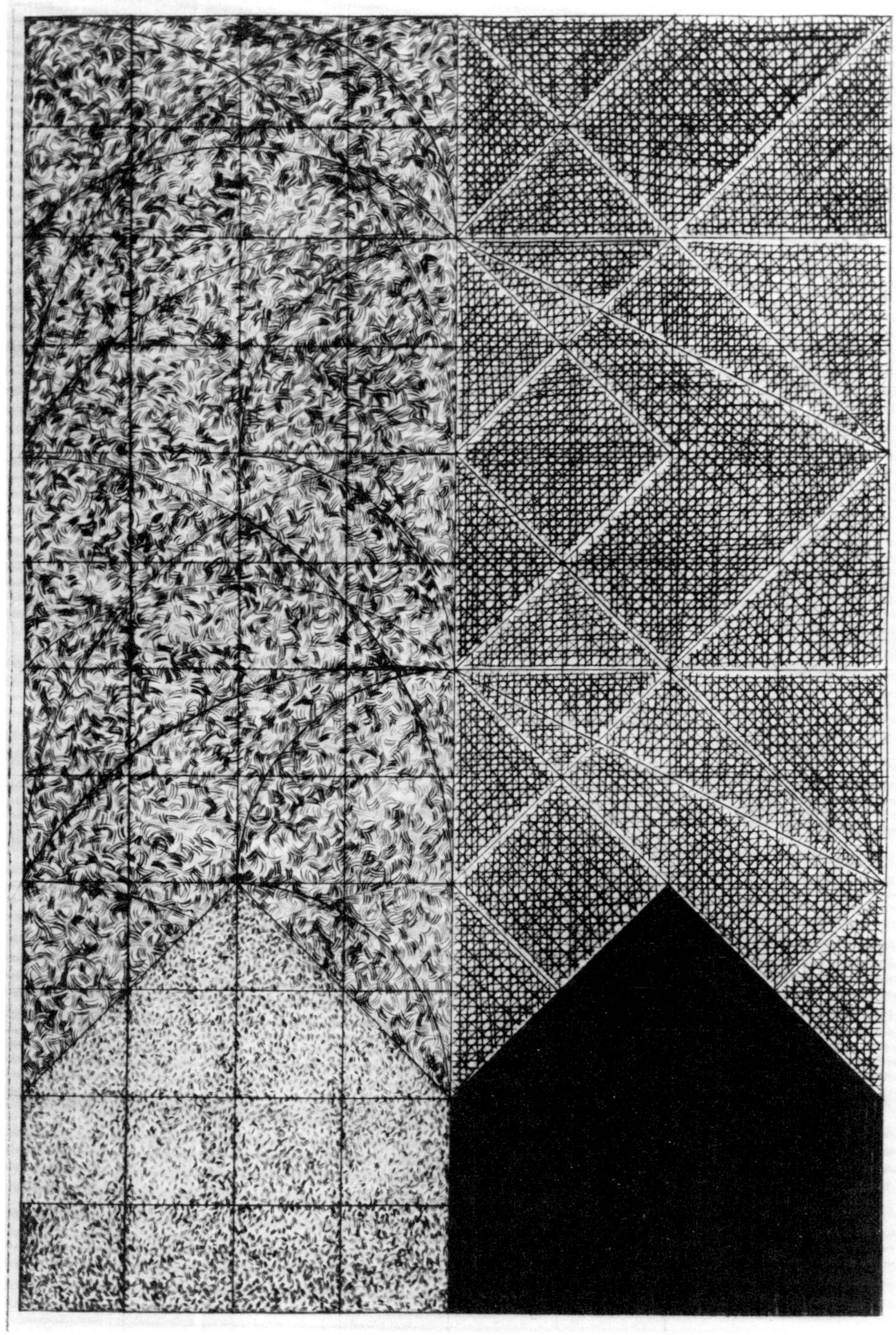

Jennifer Bartlett, *Day and Night I*, 1978.

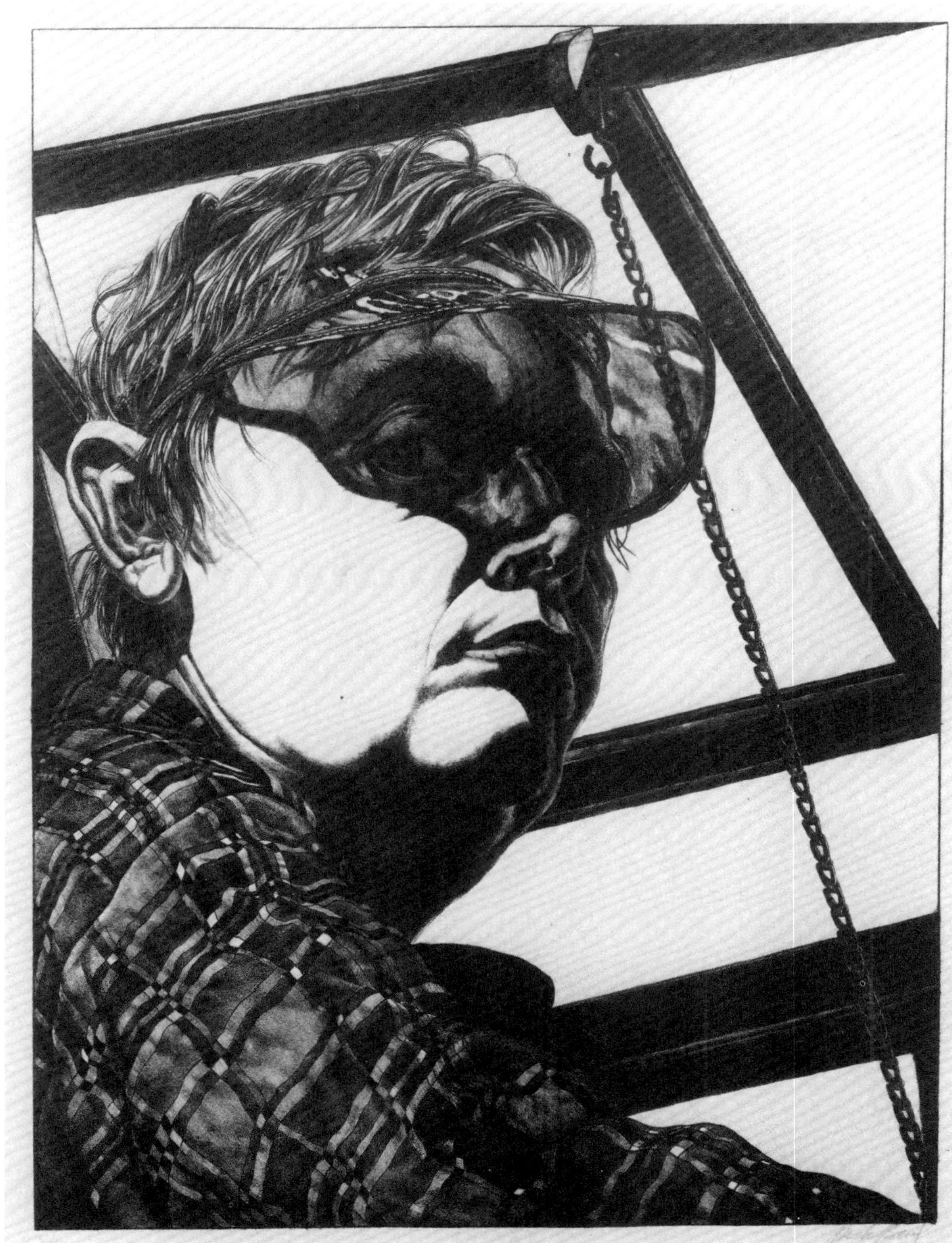

Jack Beal, *Self-Portrait*, 1974–75.

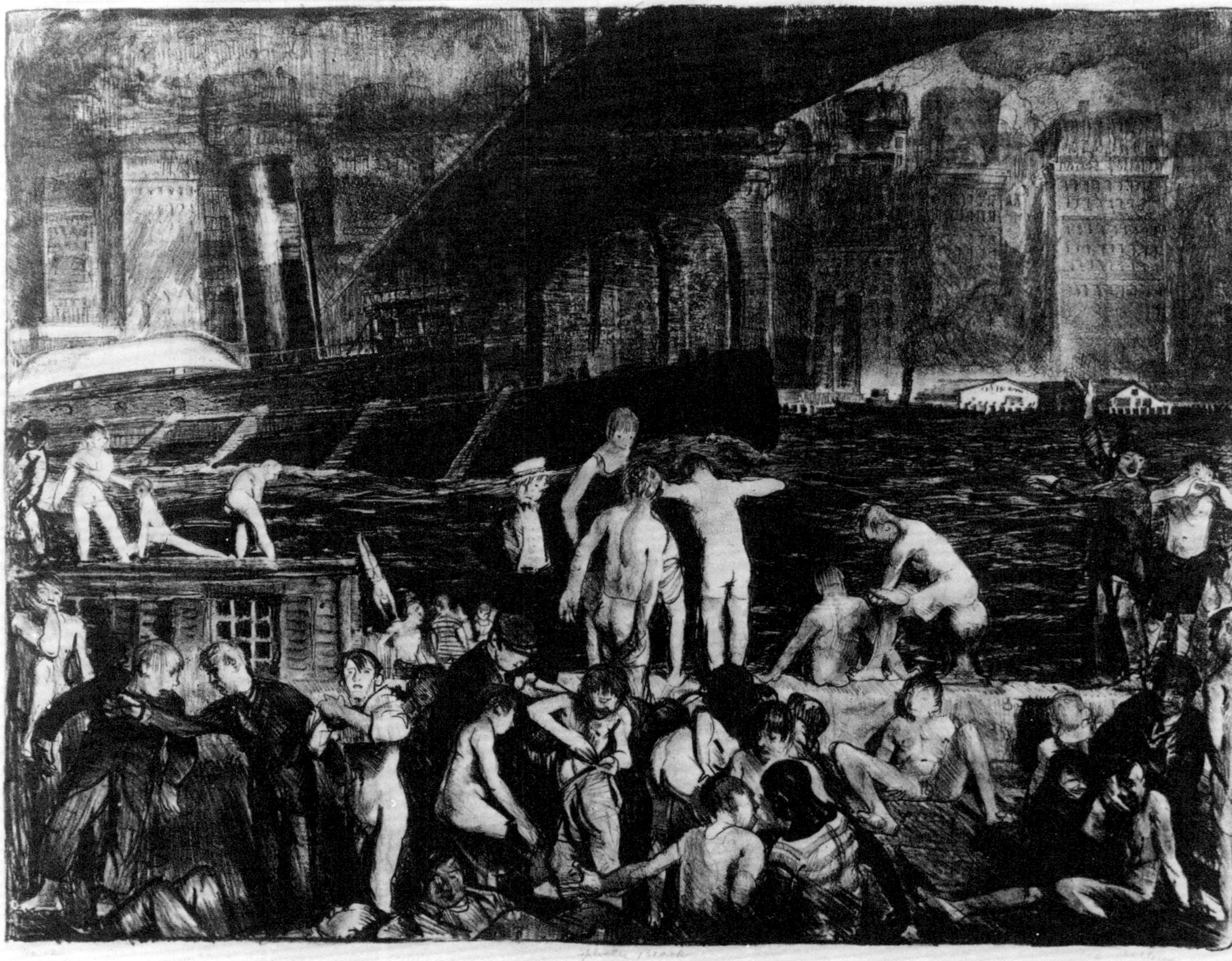

George Bellows, *Splinter Beach*, 1916.

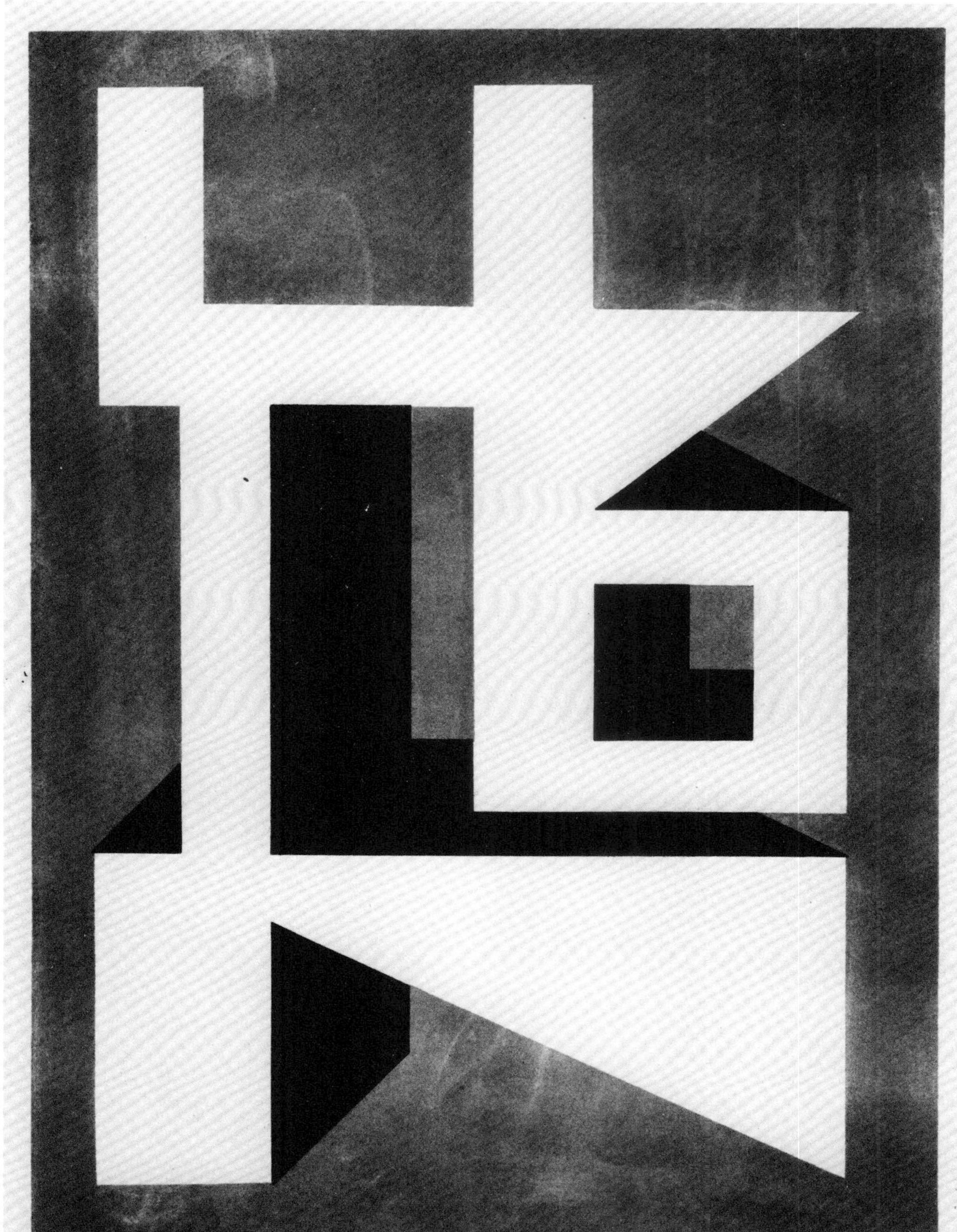

Charles Biederman, *Study for Color Sculpture Outdoors, New York*, 1937.

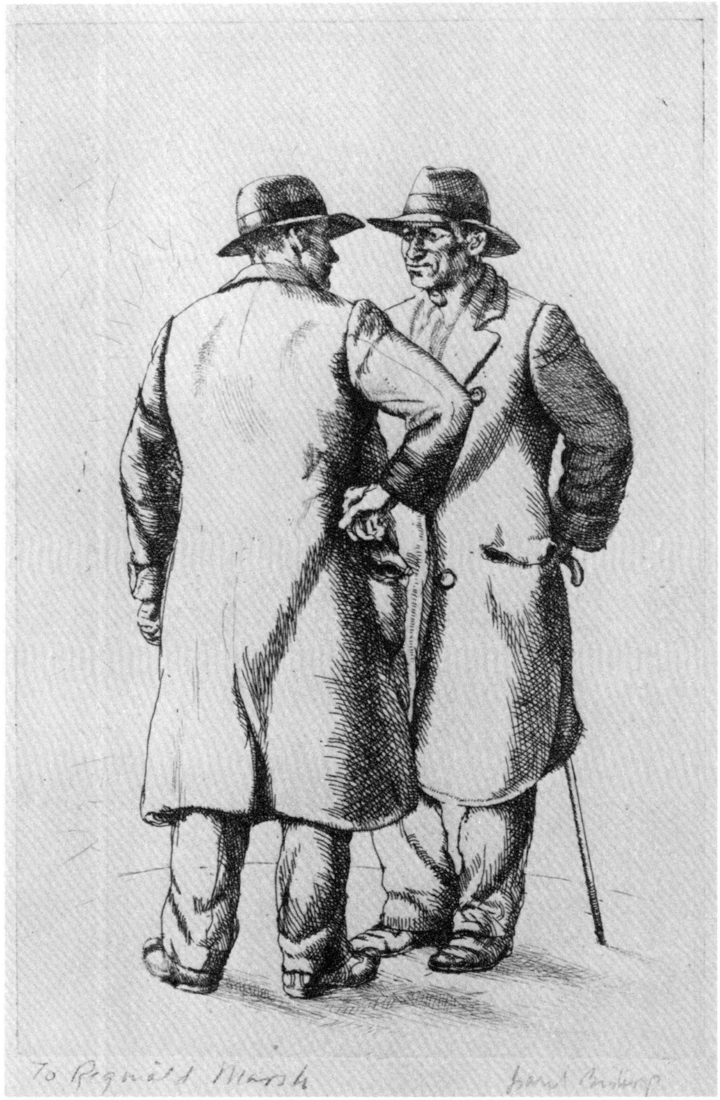

Isabel Bishop, *Conversation*, 1931.

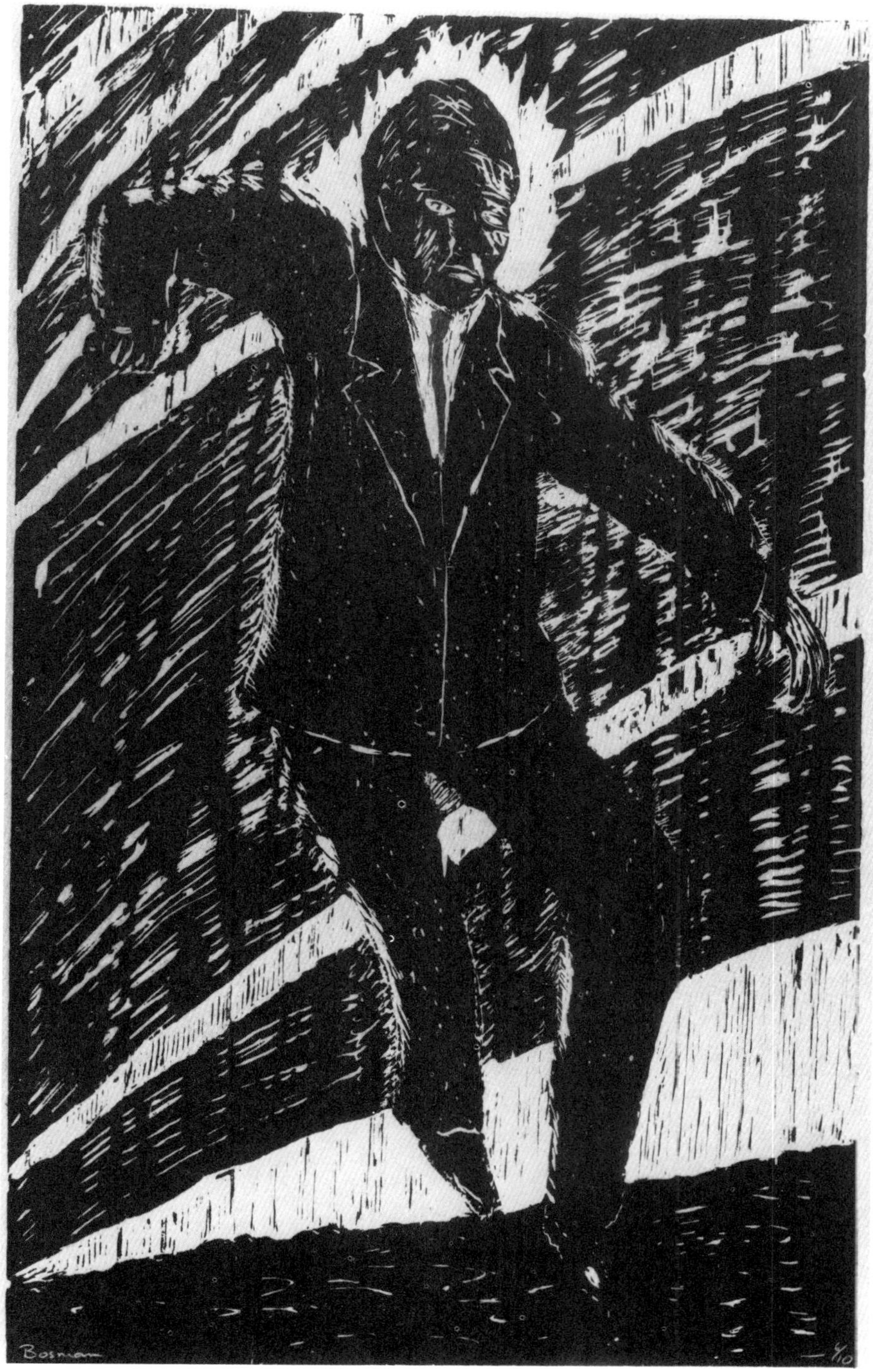

Richard Bosman, *Survivor*, 1982–83.

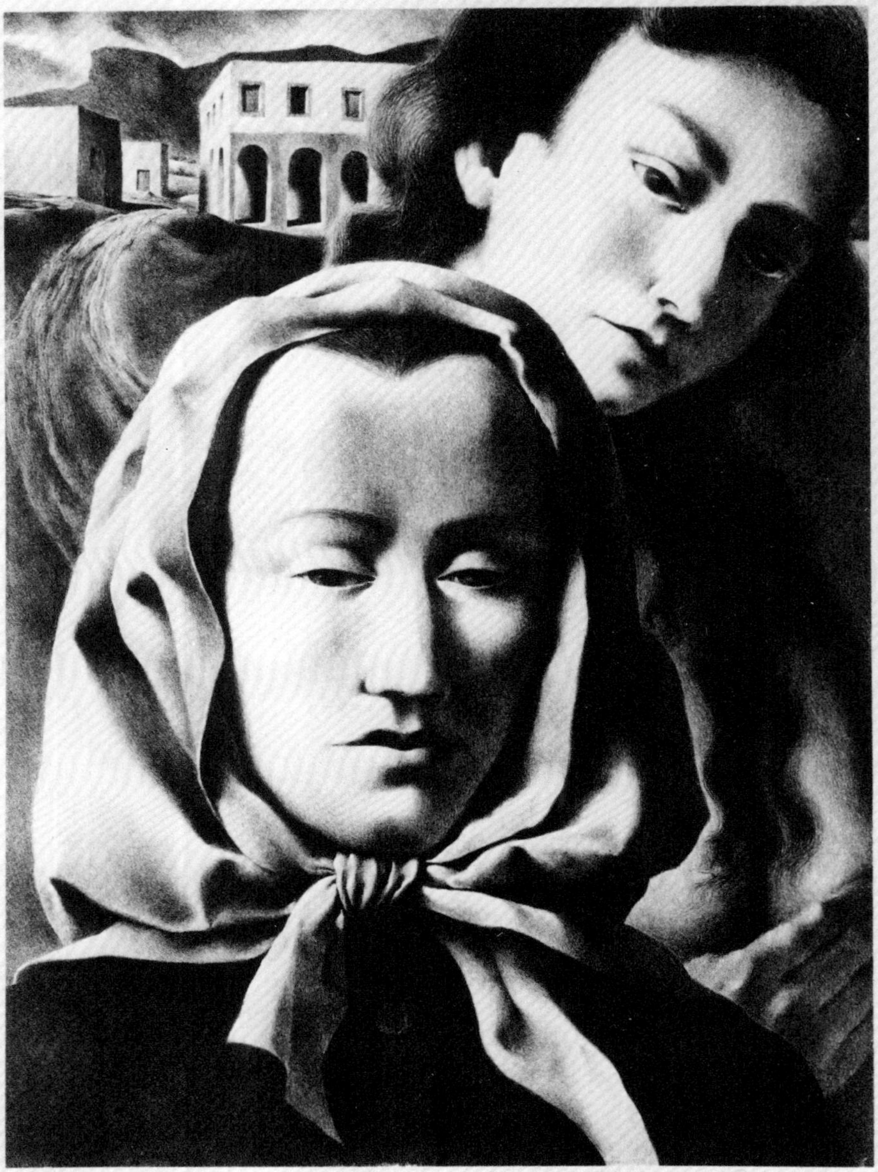

Federico Castellon, *Memories*, c. 1940.

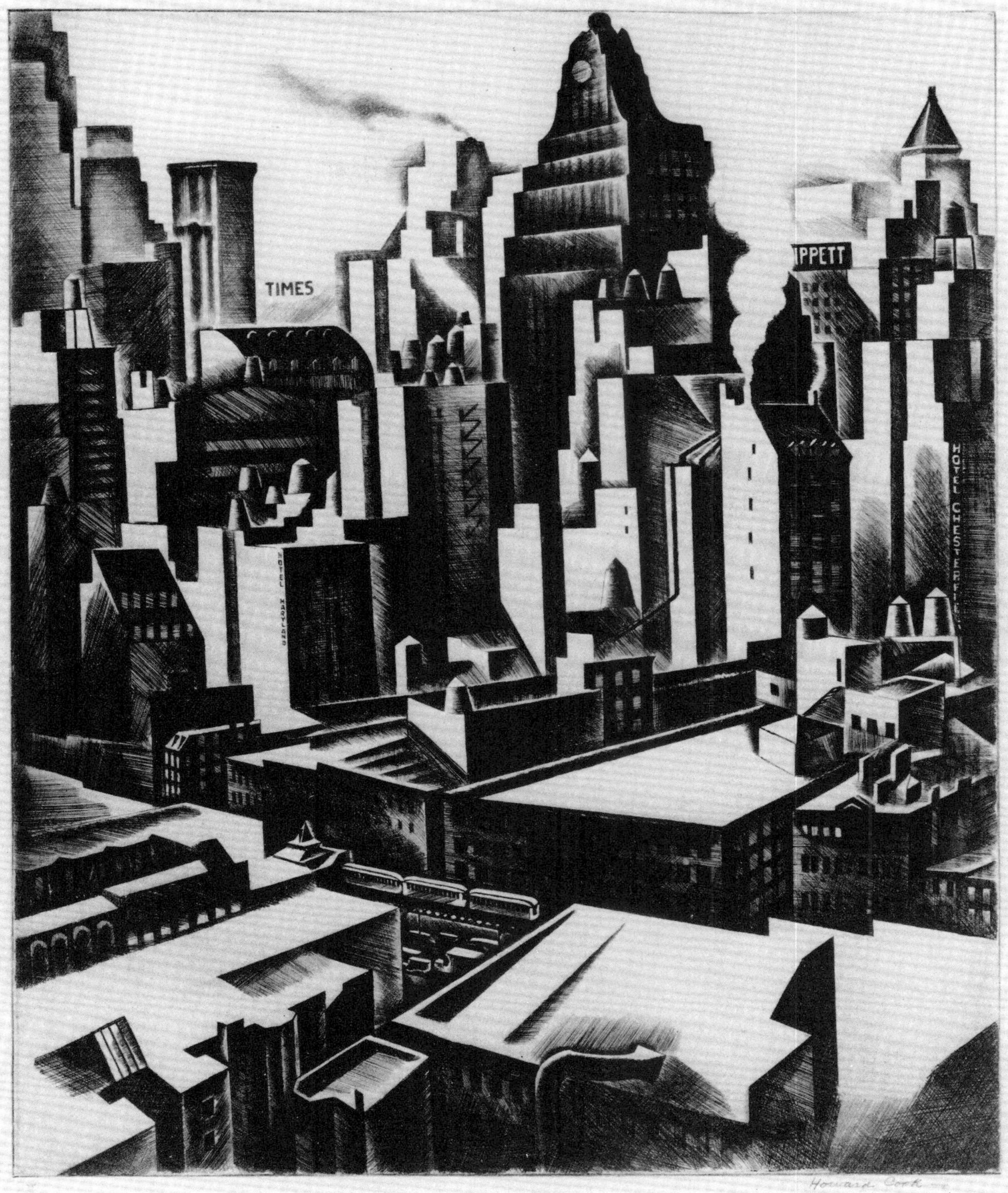

Howard Cook, *Times Square Sector*, 1930.

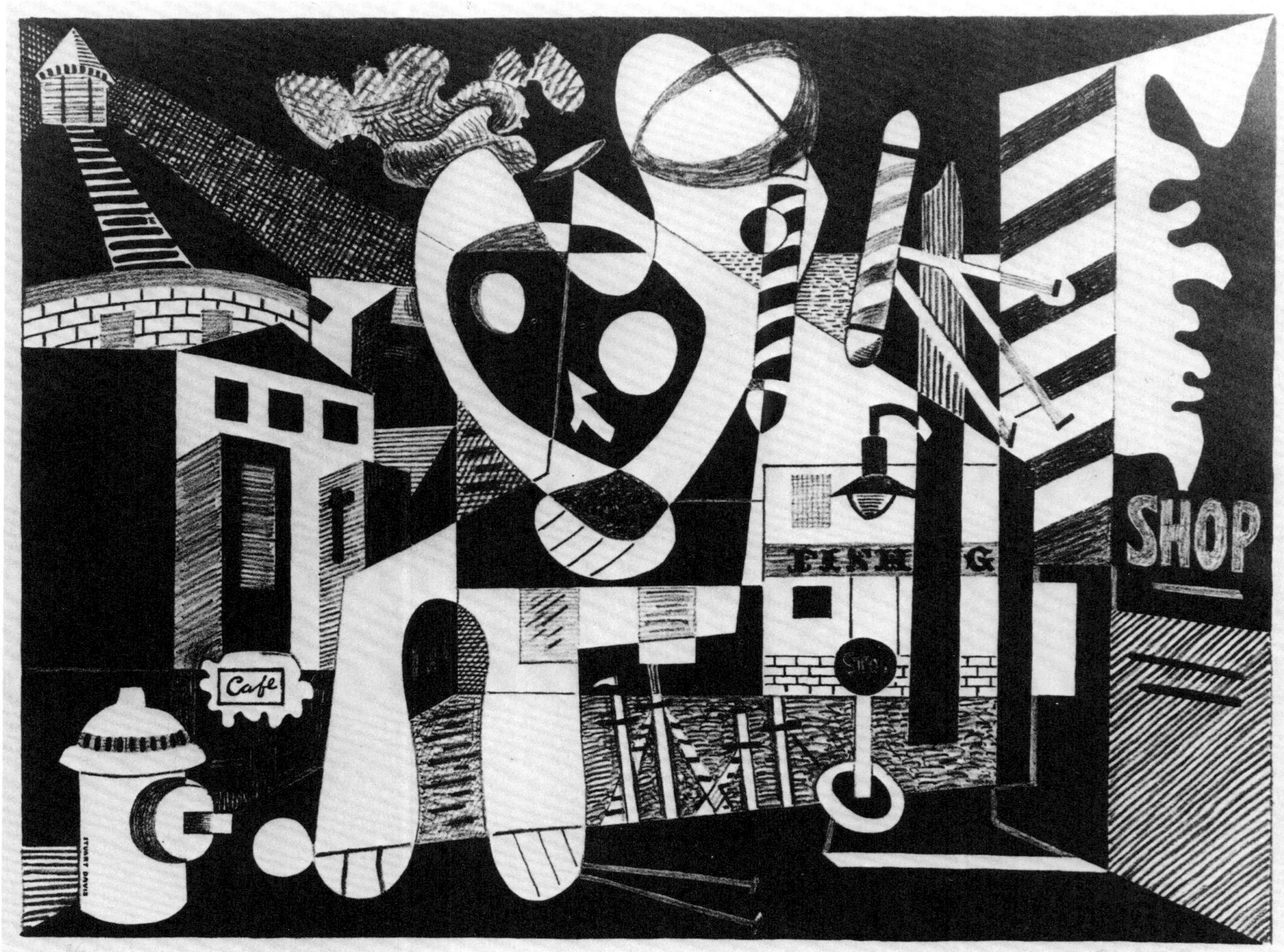

Stuart Davis, *Barber Shop Chord*, 1931.

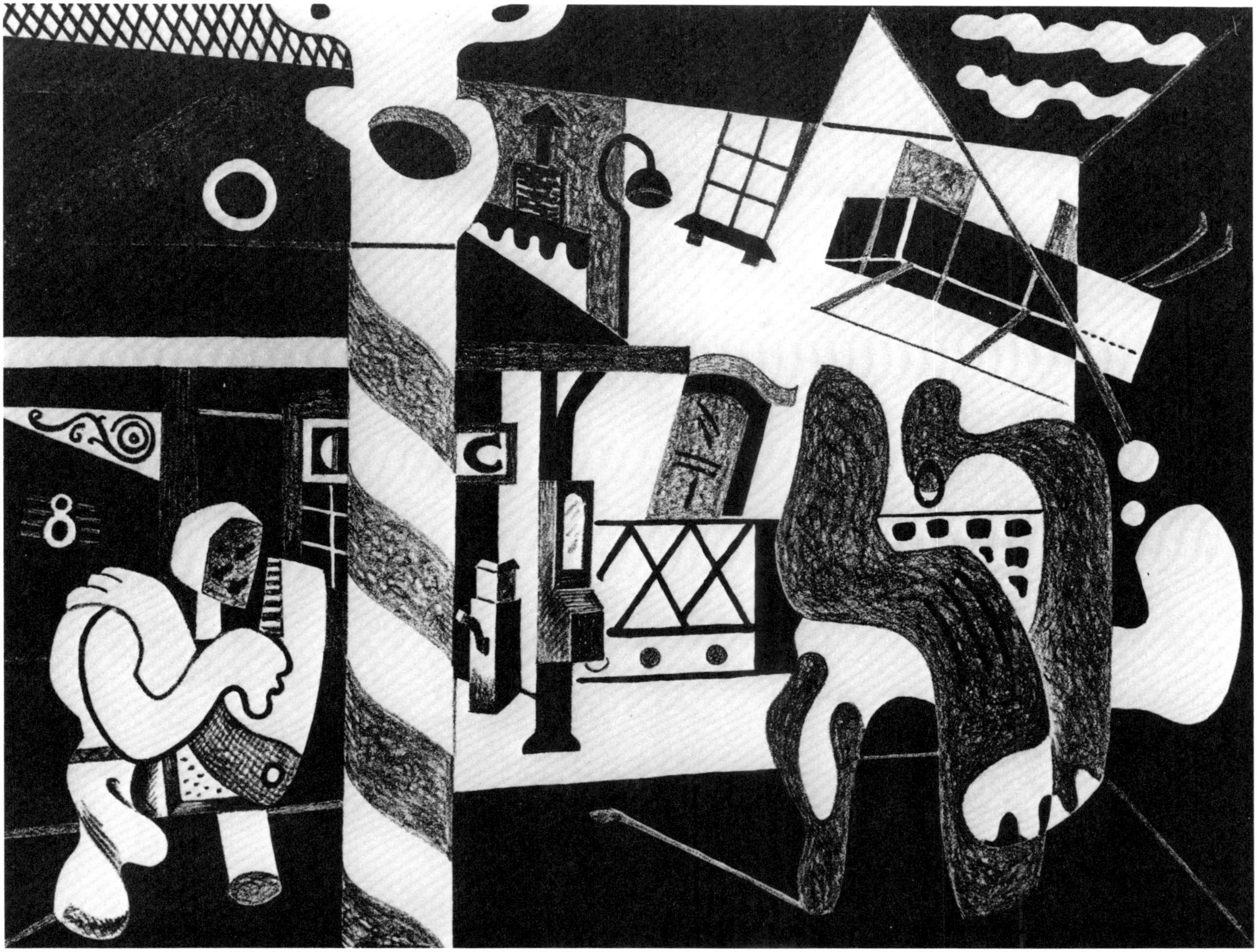

Stuart Davis, *Two Figures and El*, 1931.

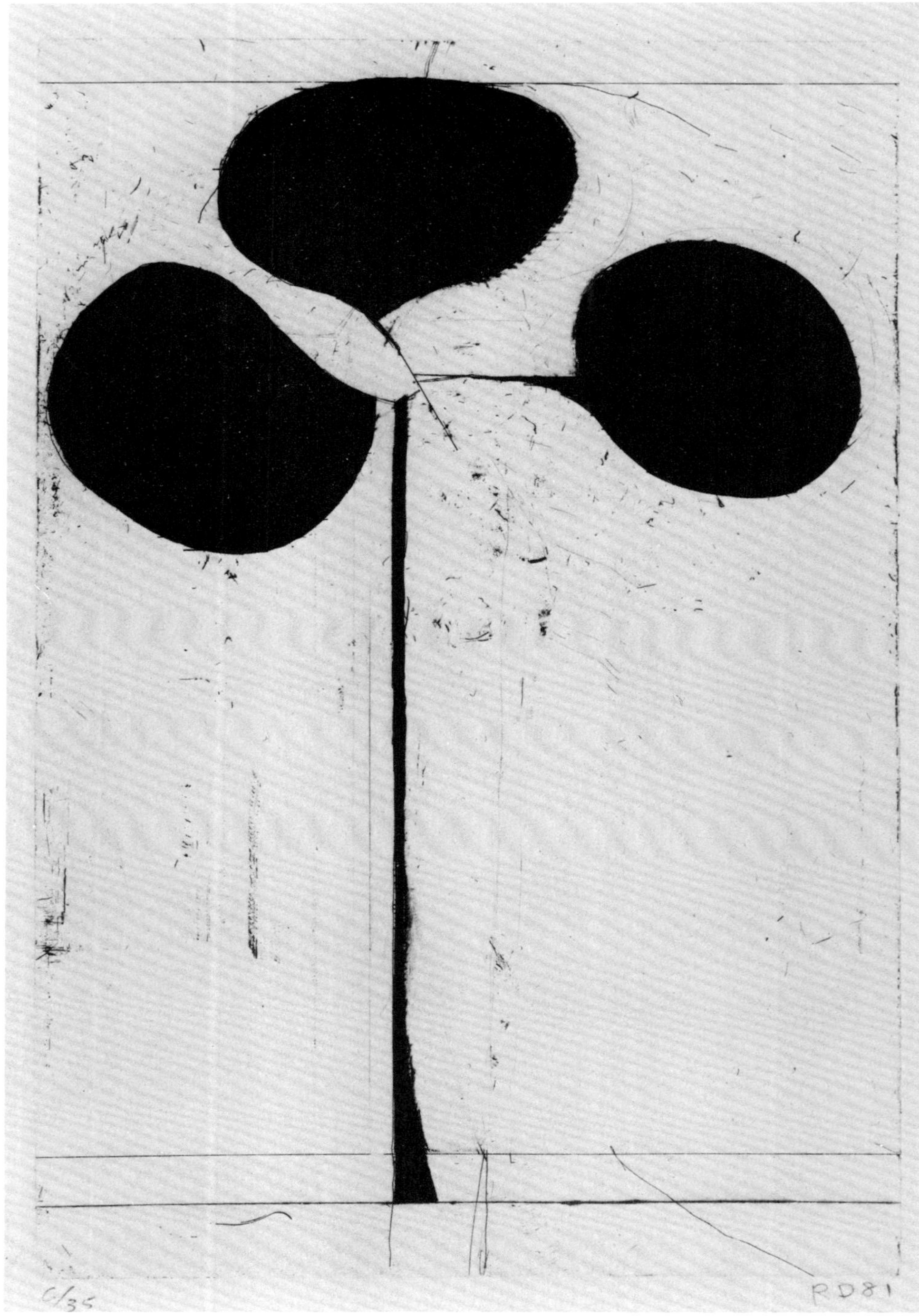

Richard Diebenkorn, *Black Club*, 1981.

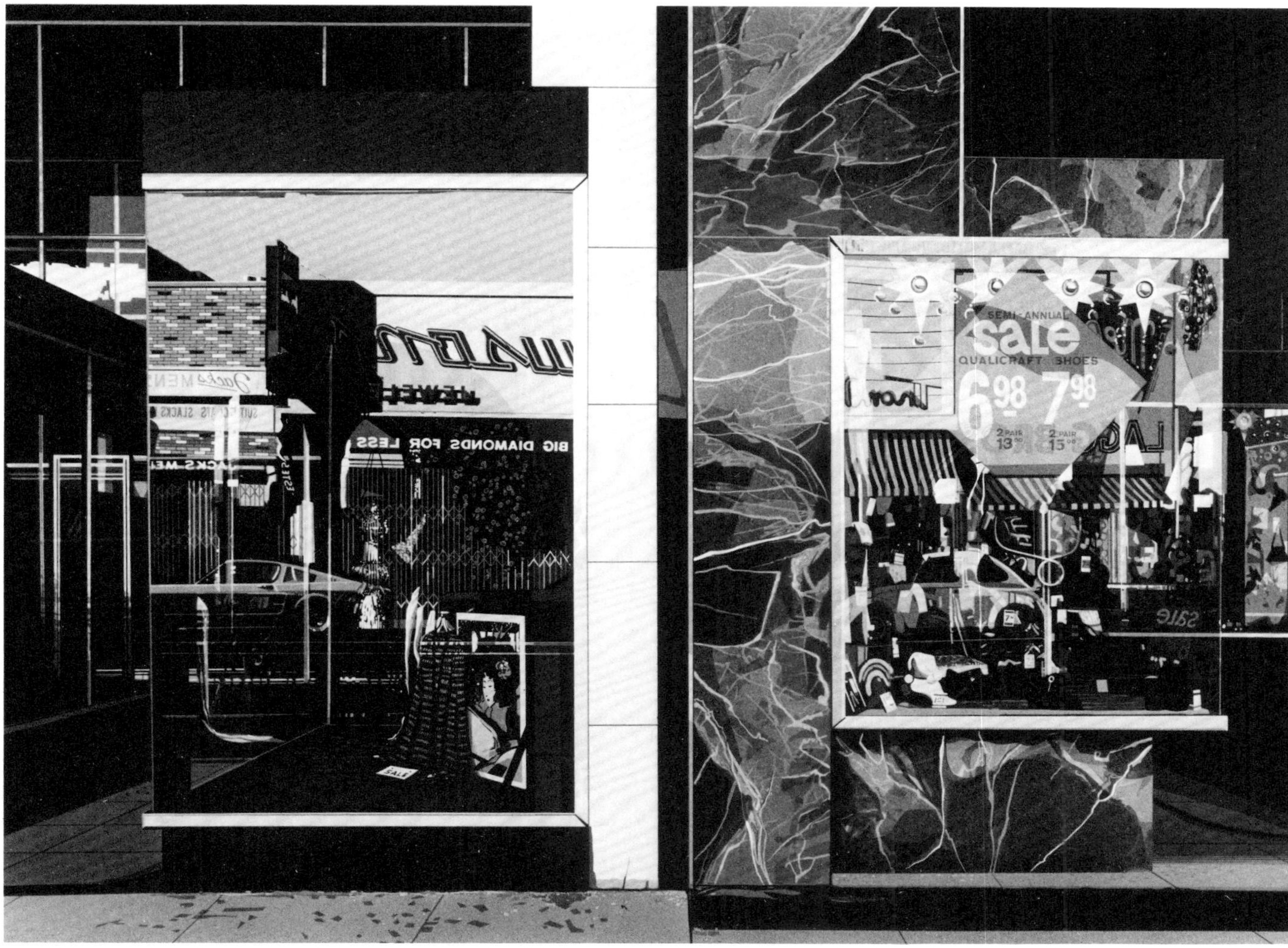

Richard Estes, *Untitled*, 1974–75.

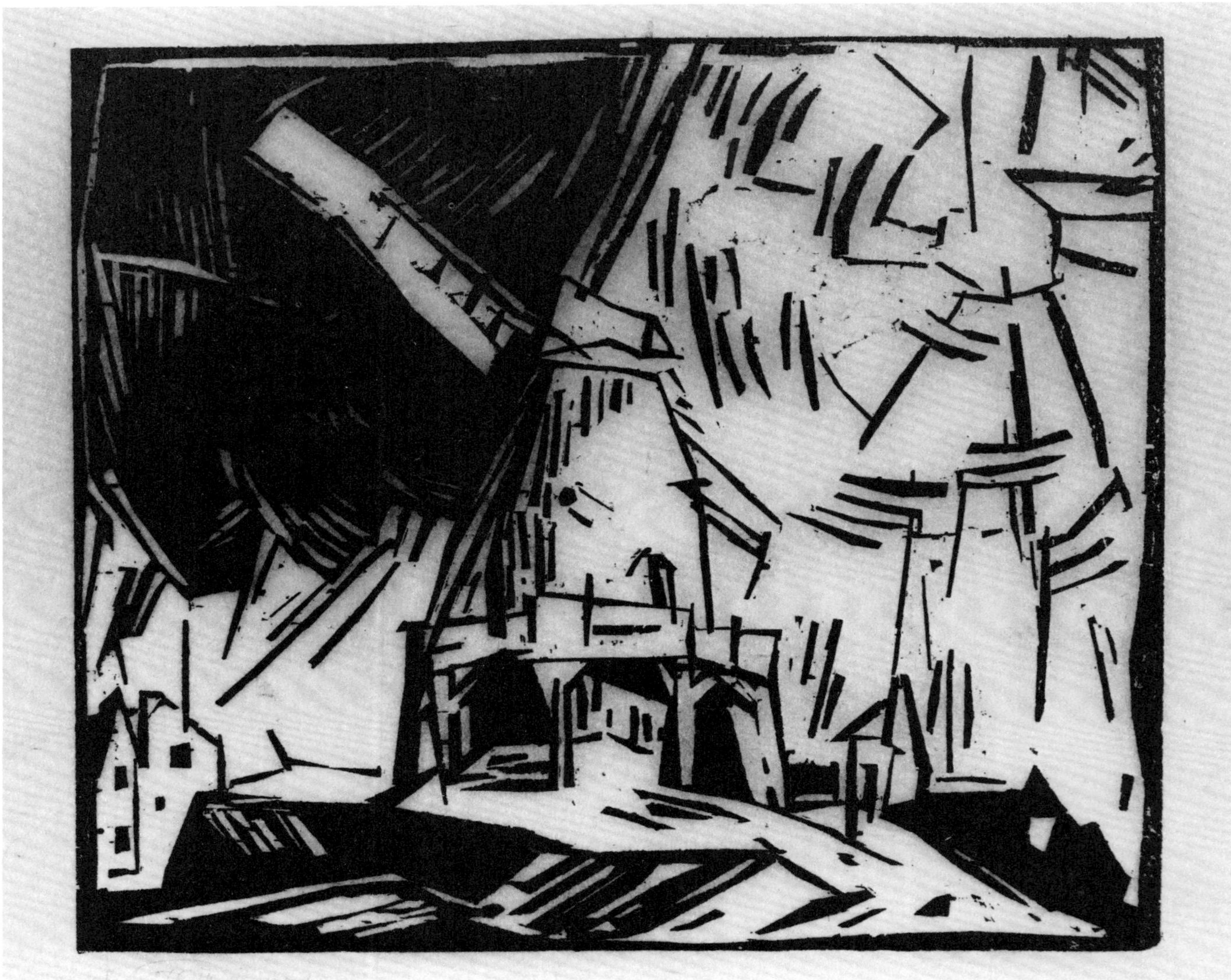

Lyonel Feininger, *Windmill*, 1919.

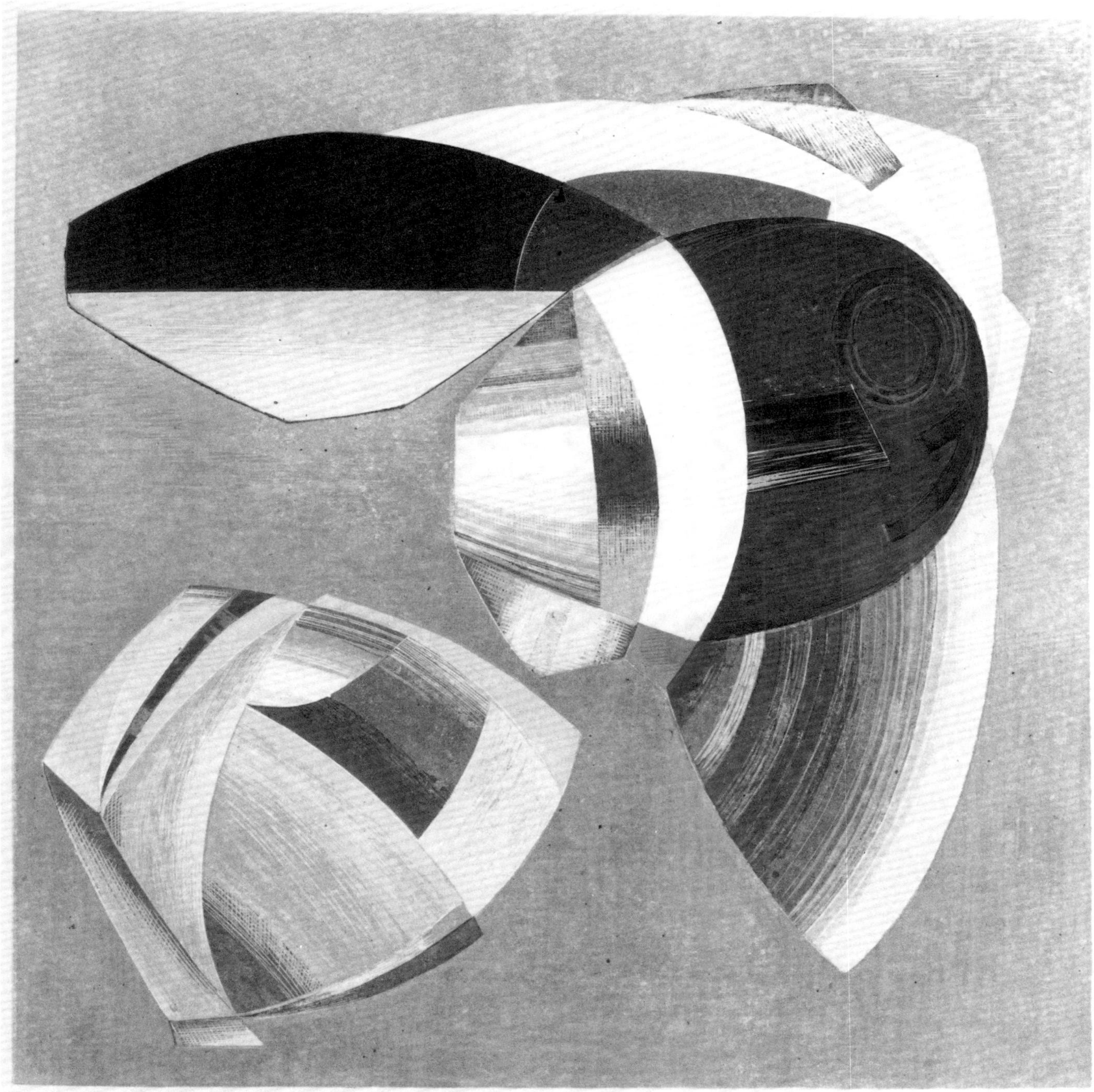

John Ferren, *Sea Forms*, 1937.

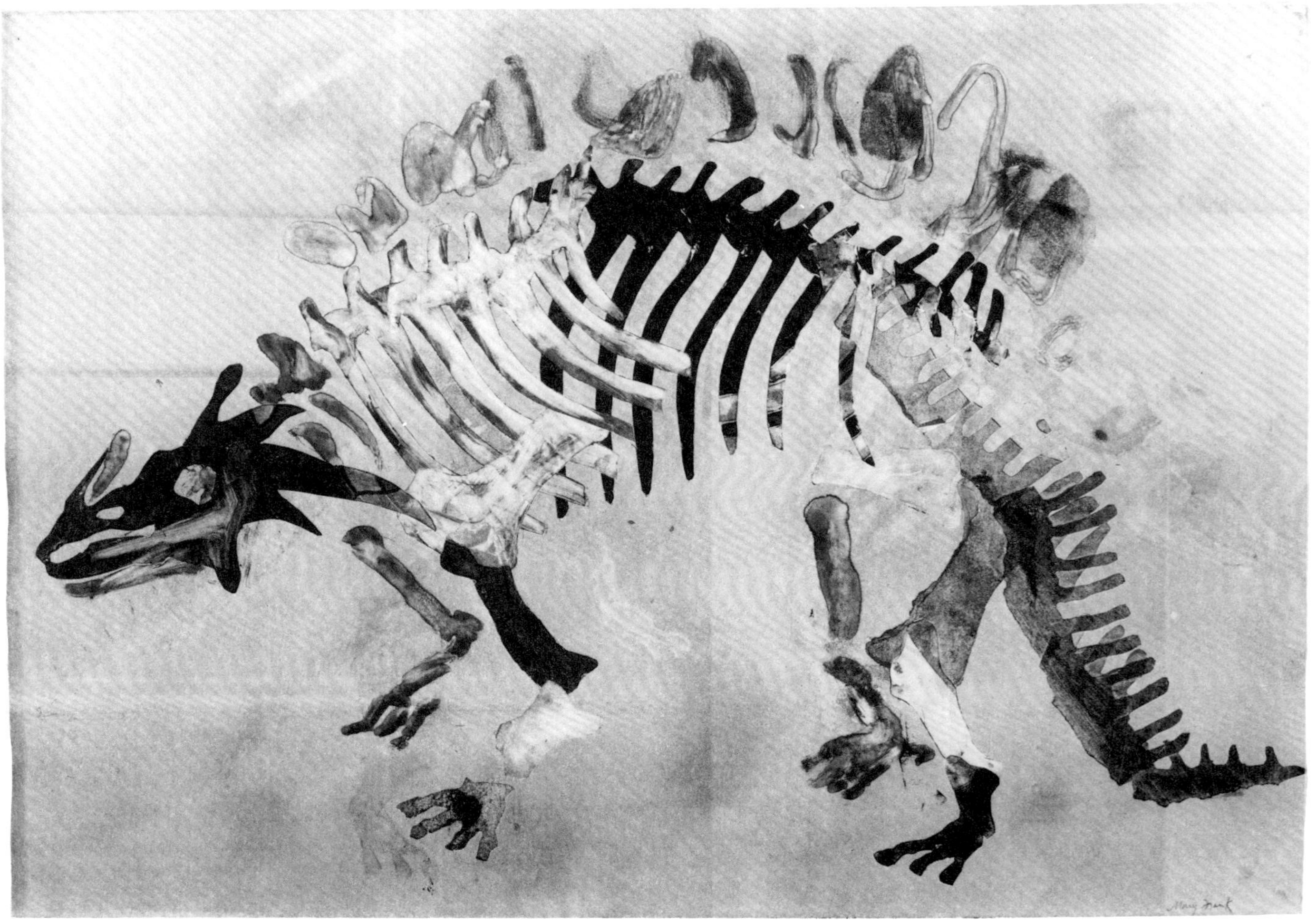

Mary Frank, *Dinosaur*, 1980.

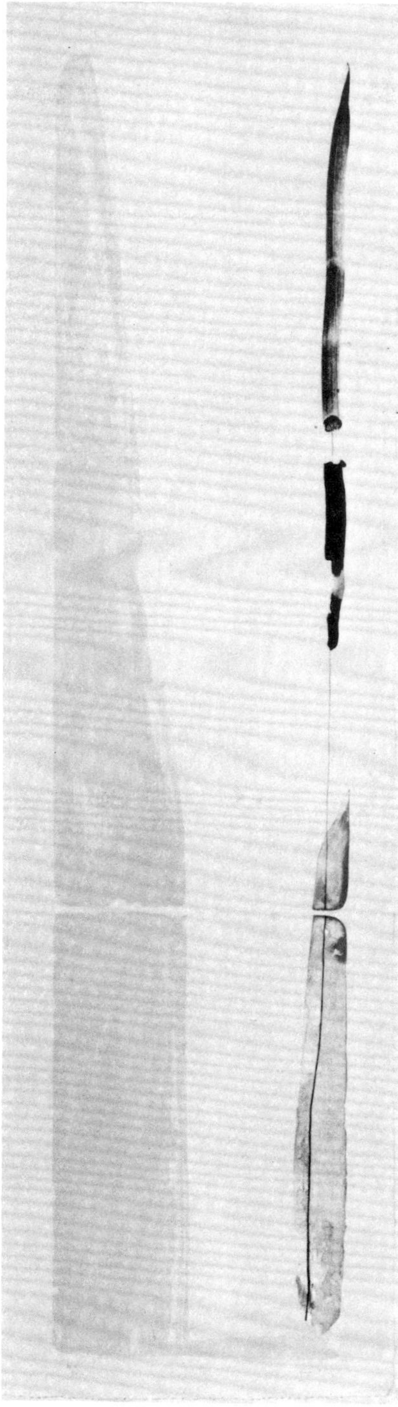

Helen Frankenthaler, *Lot's Wife*, 1971.

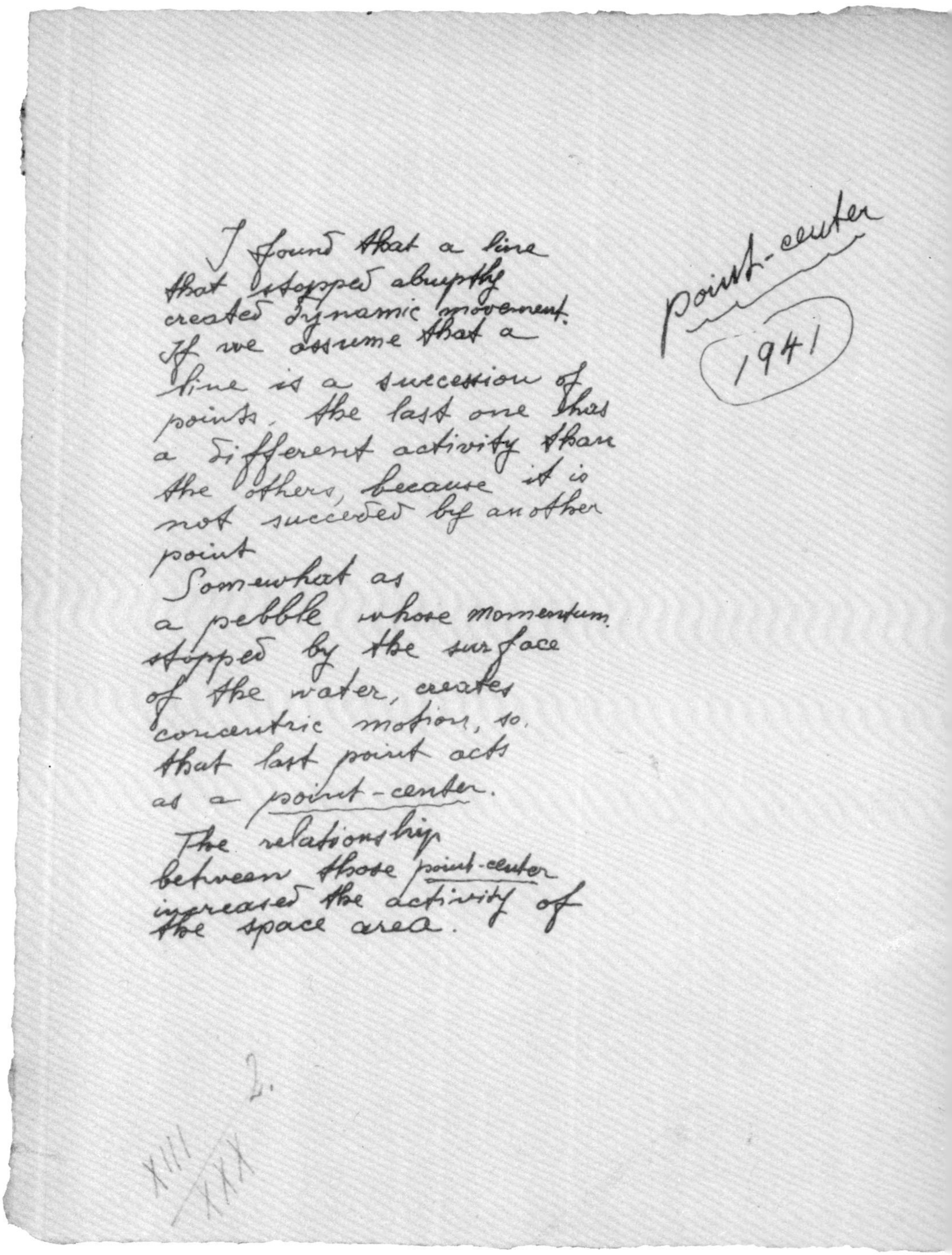

I found that a line
that stopped abruptly
created dynamic movement.
If we assume that a
line is a succession of
points, the last one has
a different activity than
the others, because it is
not succeeded by another
point
Somewhat as
a pebble whose momentum
stopped by the surface
of the water, creates
concentric motion, so
that last point acts
as a point-center.
The relationship
between those point-center
increased the activity of
the space area.

point-center

1941

2.

XIII
XXX

Fritz Glarner, *Recollection*, from the book *Recollection*, 1964–68.

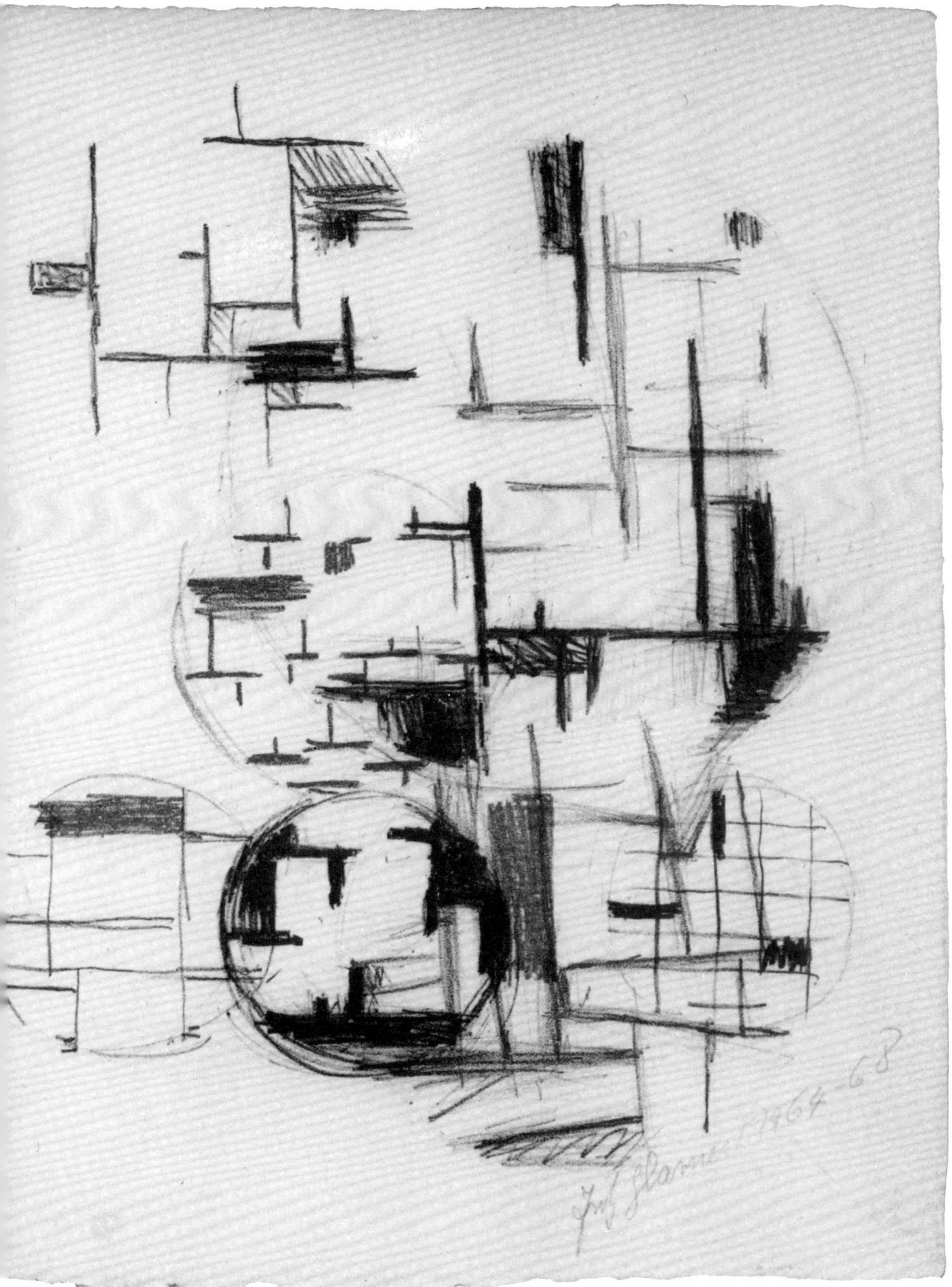

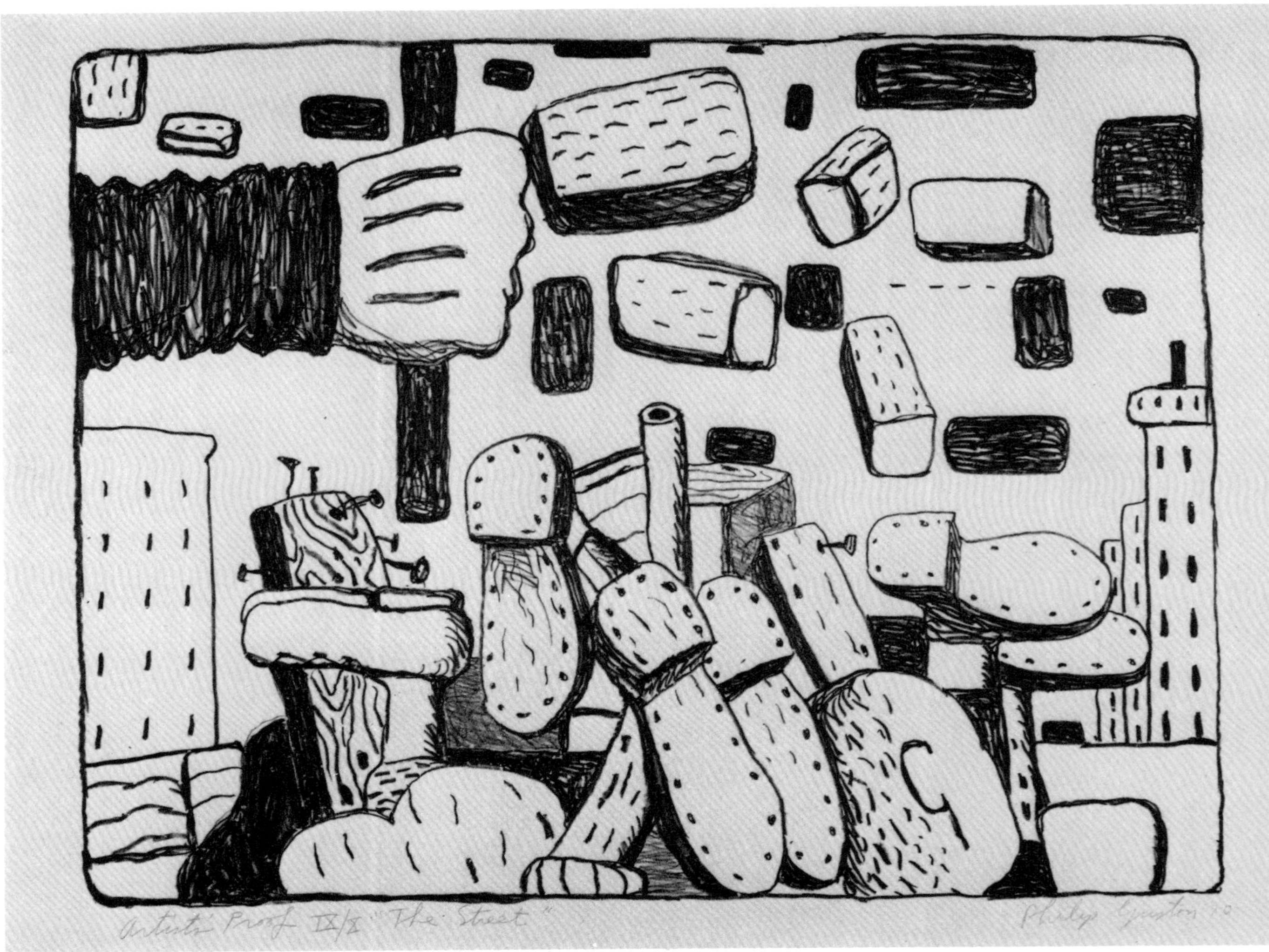

Philip Guston, *The Street*, 1970.

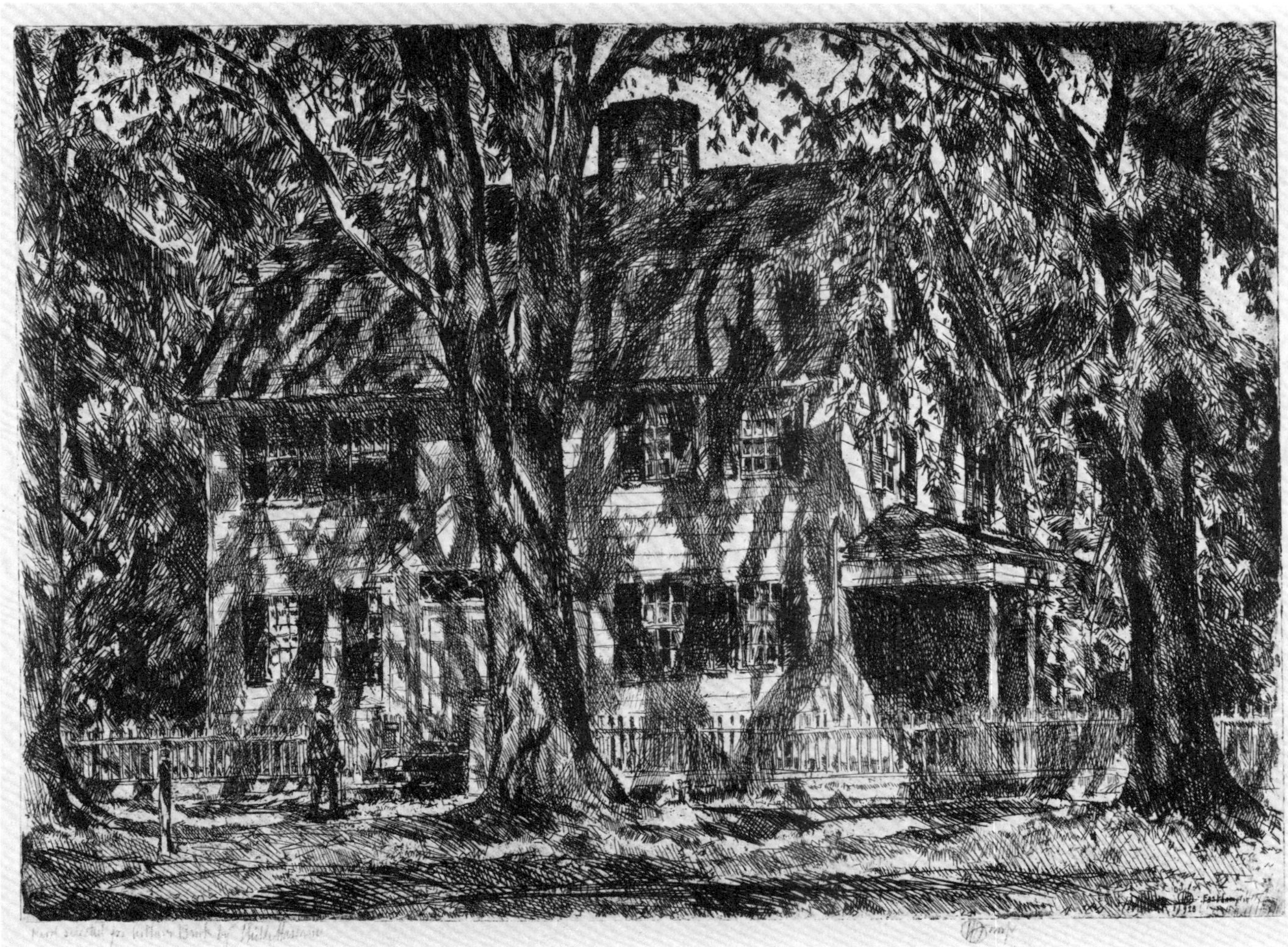

Childe Hassam, *The Lion Gardiner House, East Hampton*, 1920.

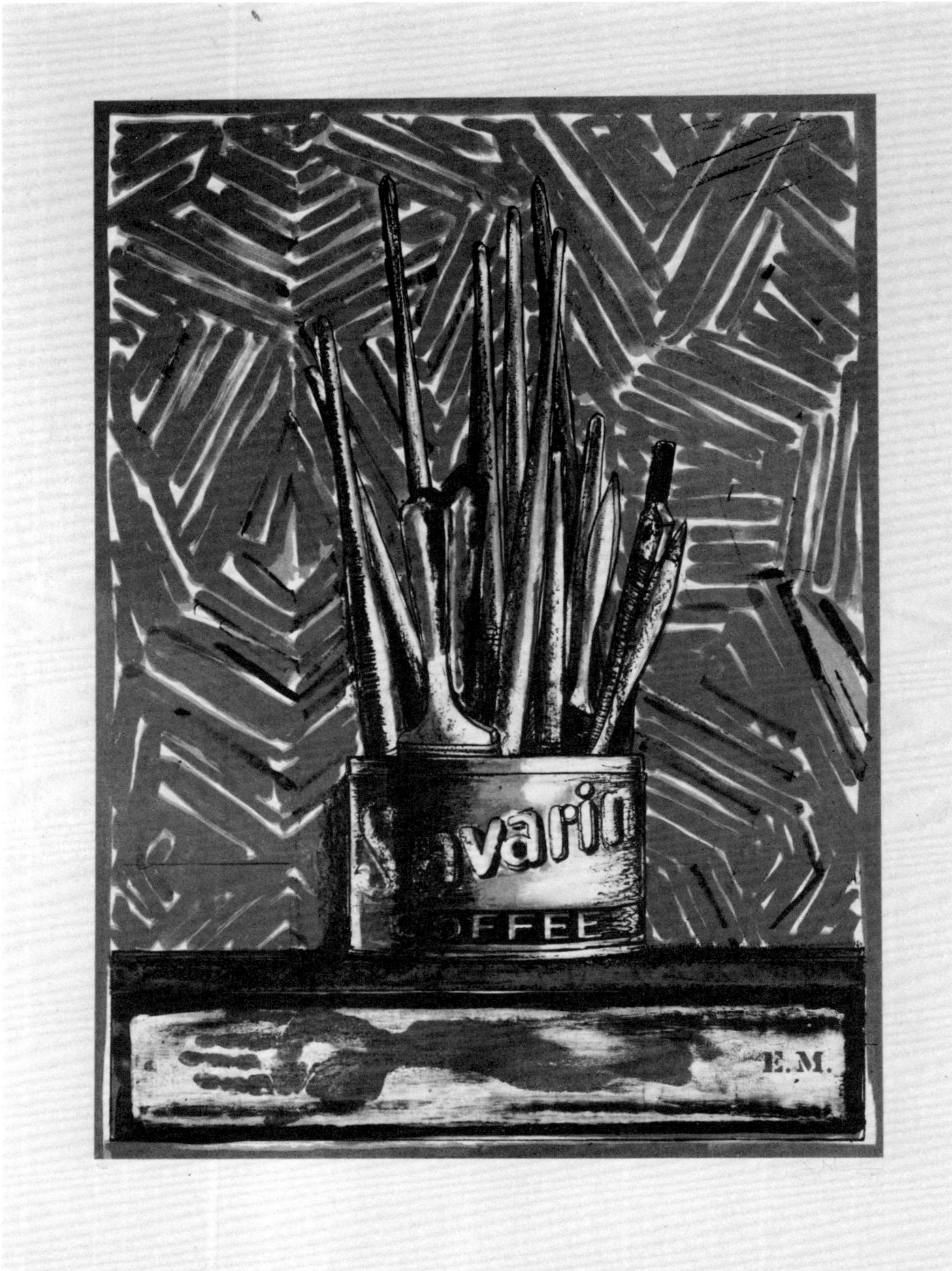

Jasper Johns, *Savarin*, 1977–81.

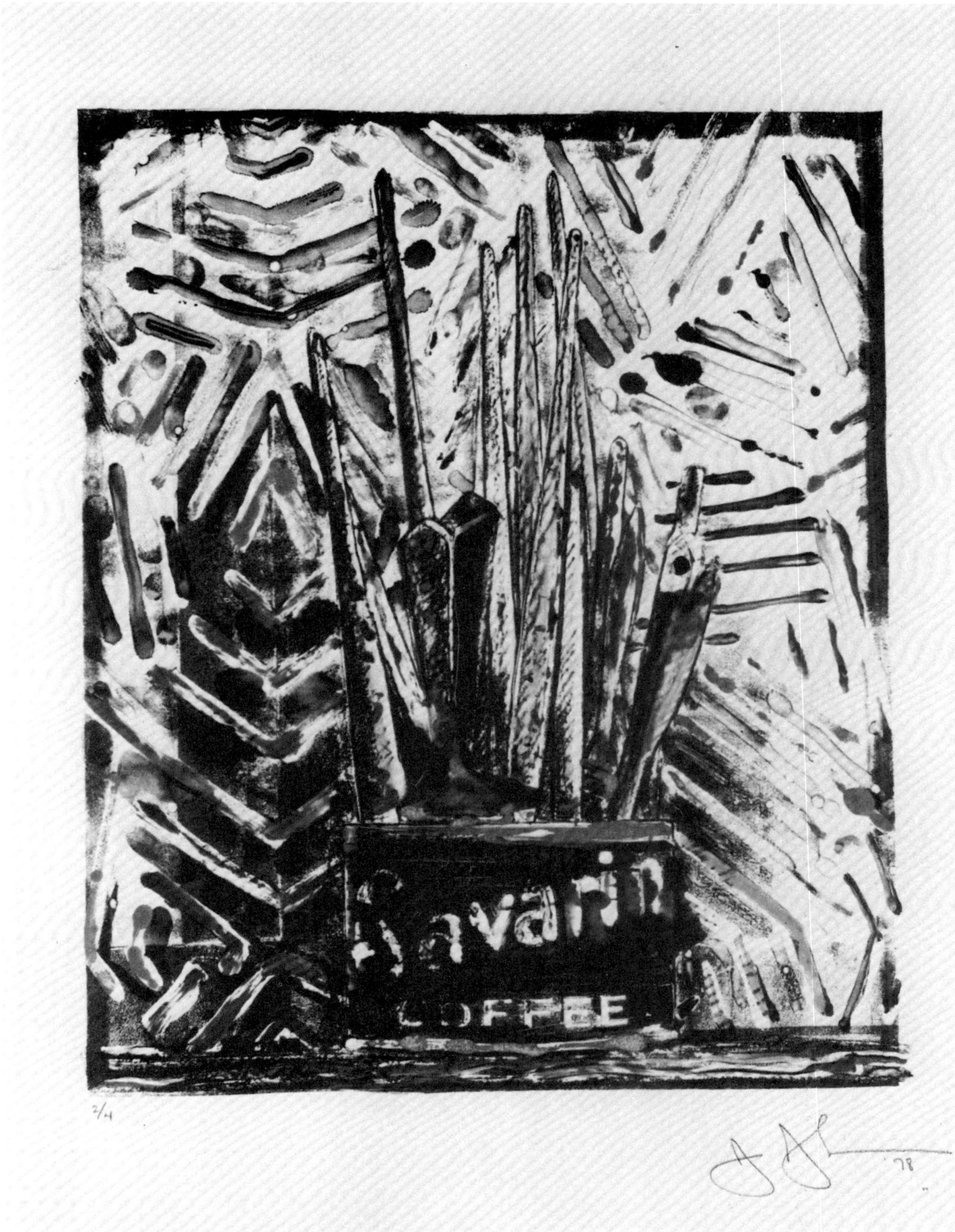

Jasper Johns, *Savarin*, 1978.

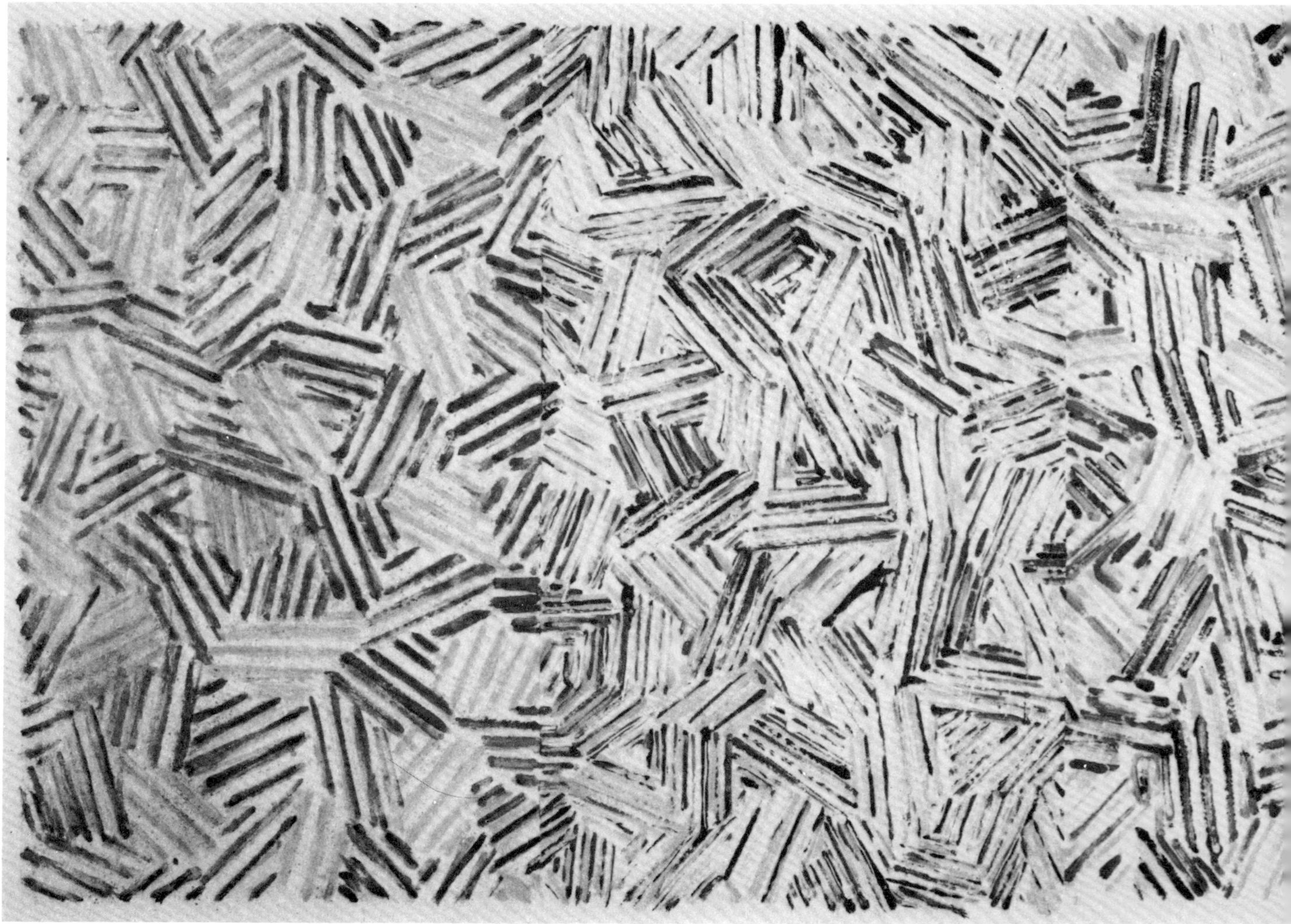

Jasper Johns, *Untitled*, 1983.

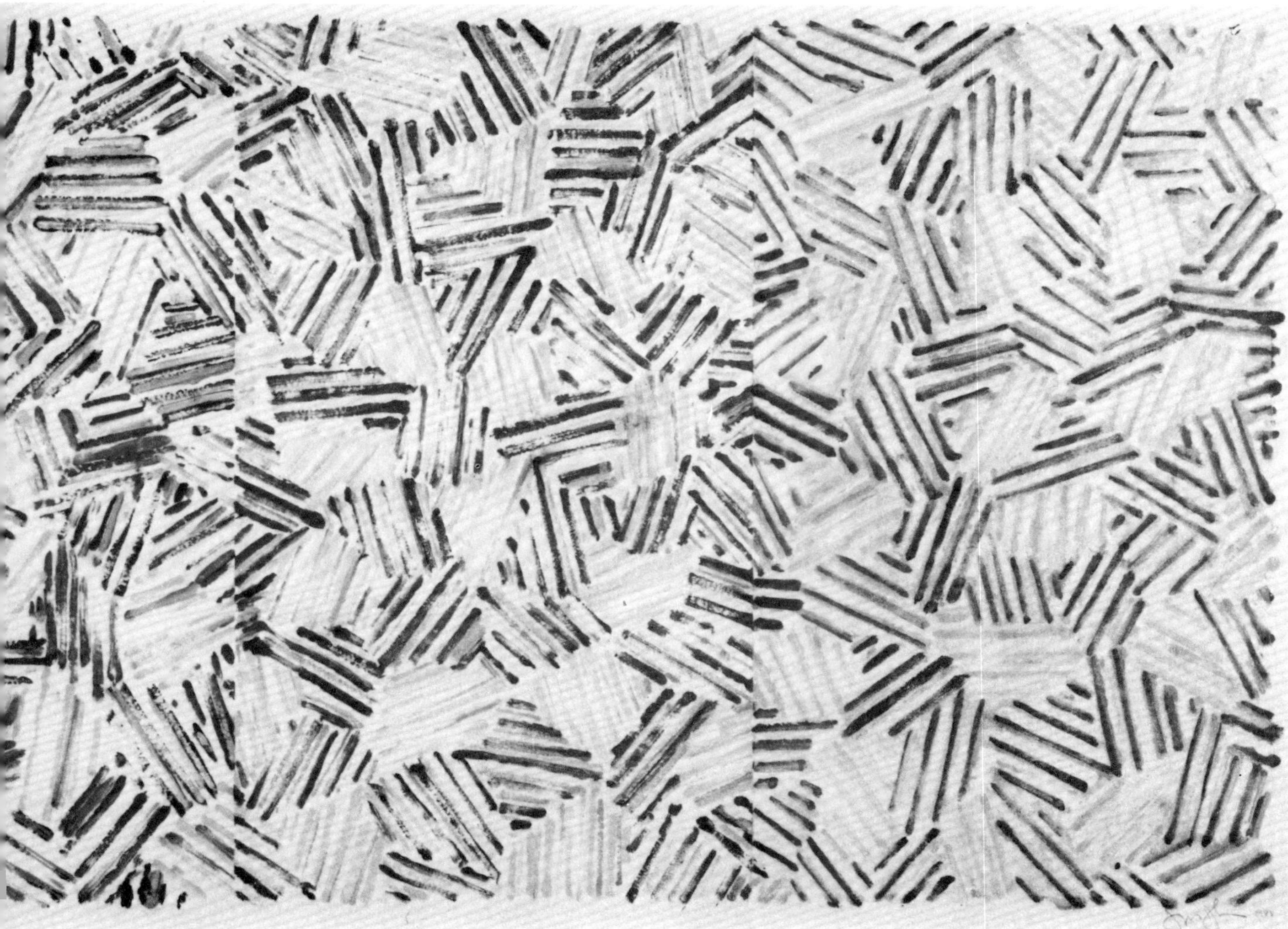

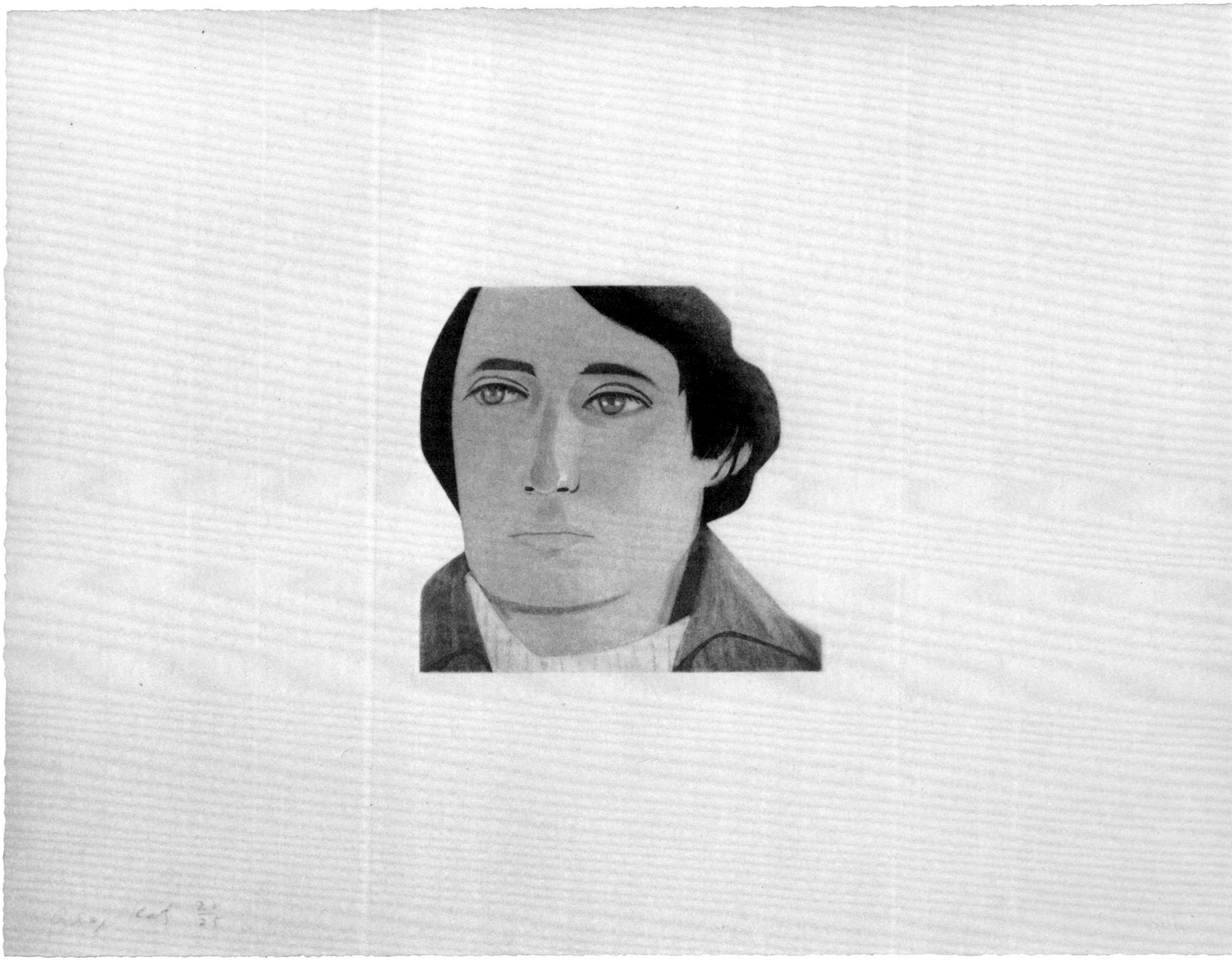

Alex Katz, *Tony Towle*, from the book *Face of the Poet*, 1978.

Ellsworth Kelly, *Wall*, 1979.

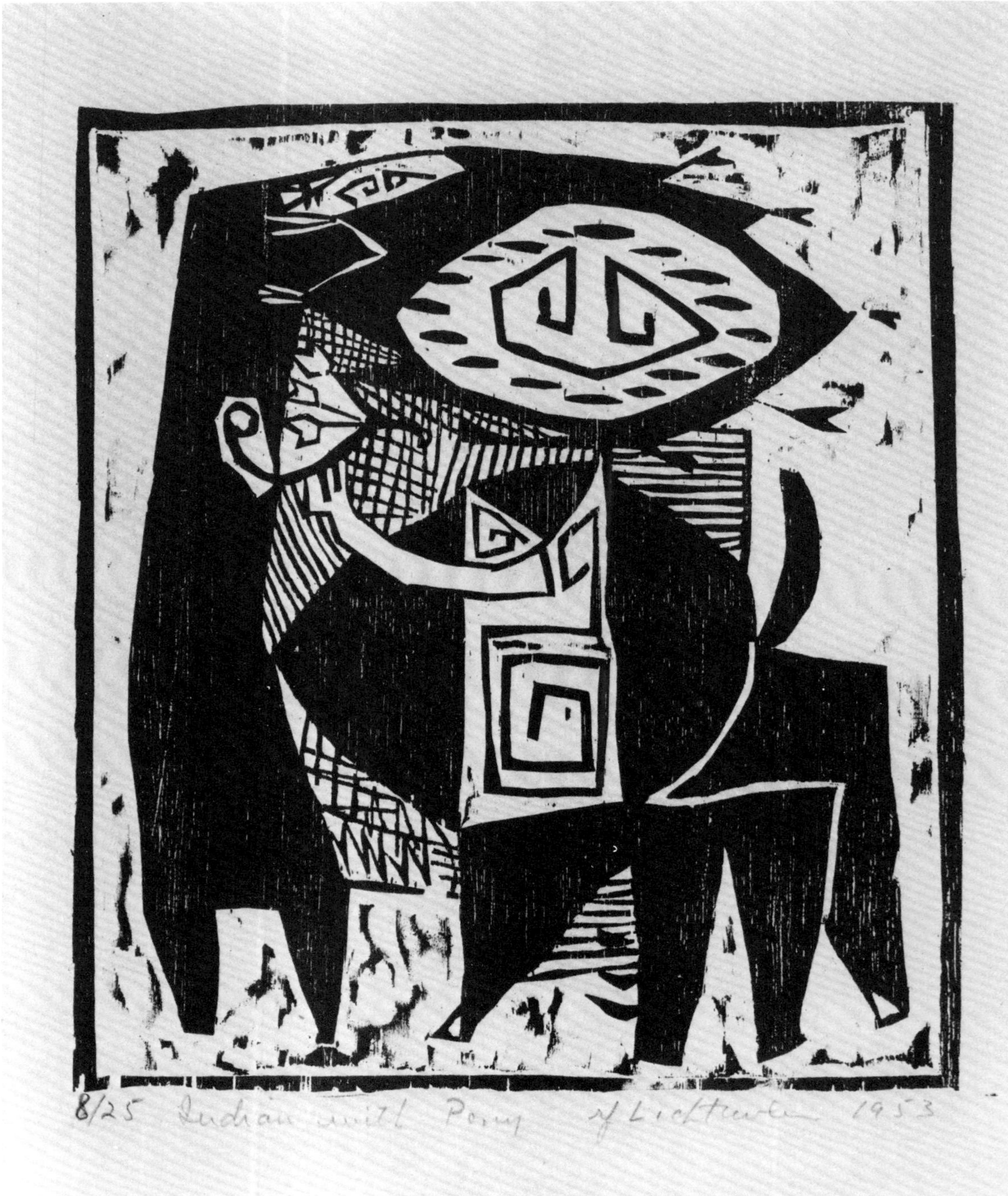

Roy Lichtenstein, *Indian with Pony*, 1953.

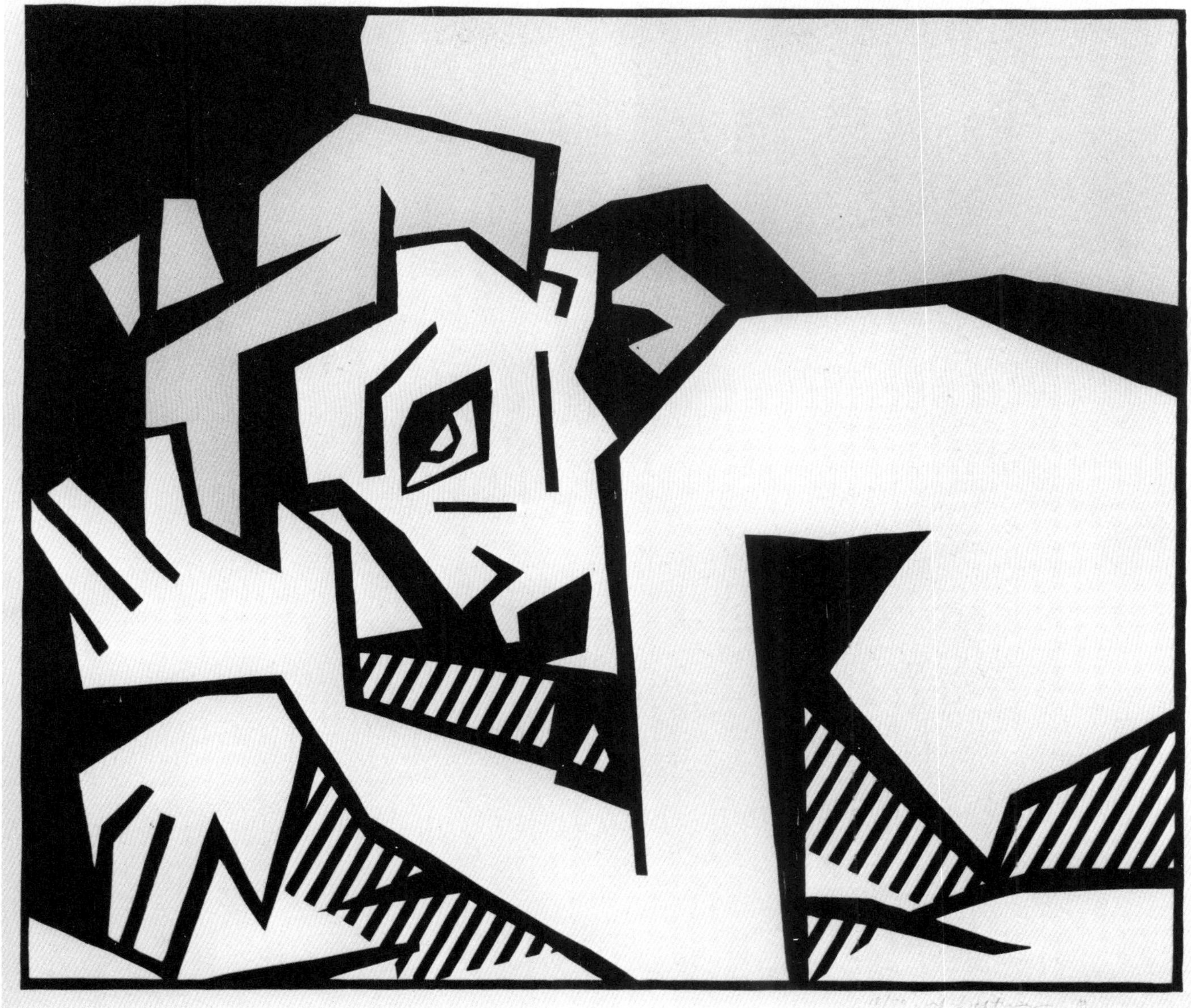

Roy Lichtenstein, *The Reclining Nude*, 1980.

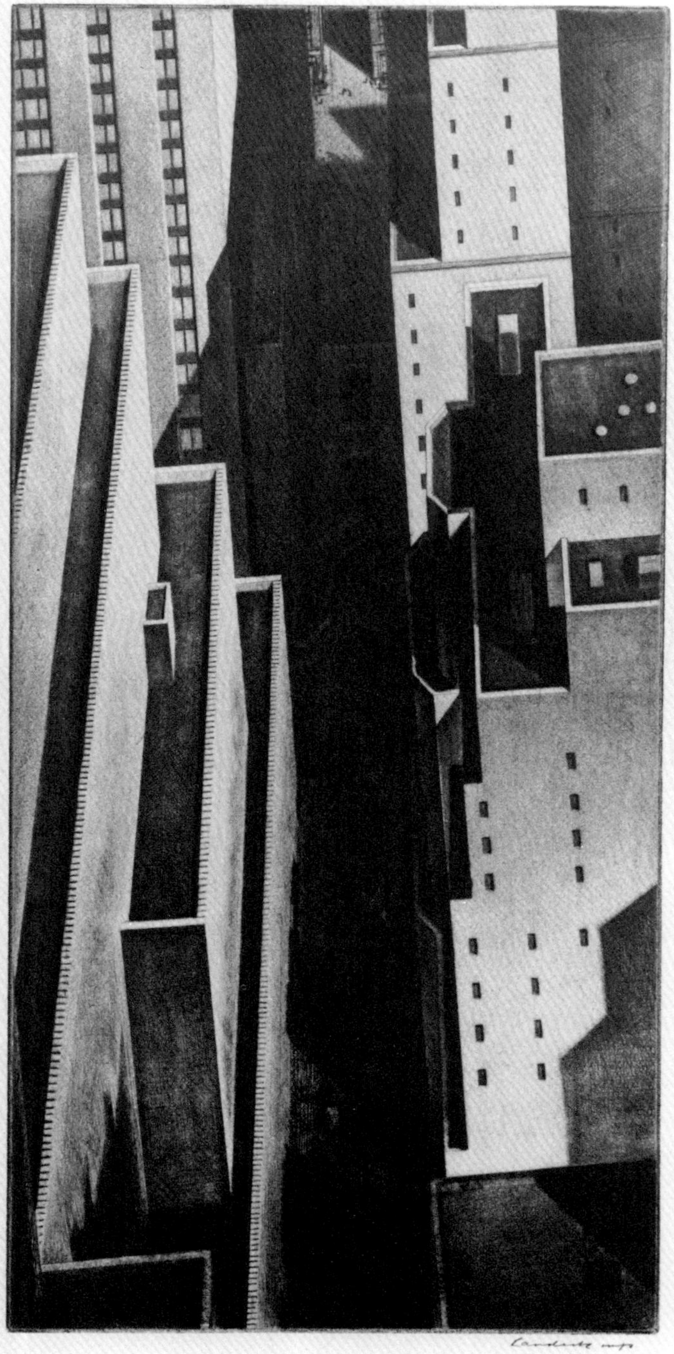

Armin Landeck, *Manhattan Canyon*, 1934.

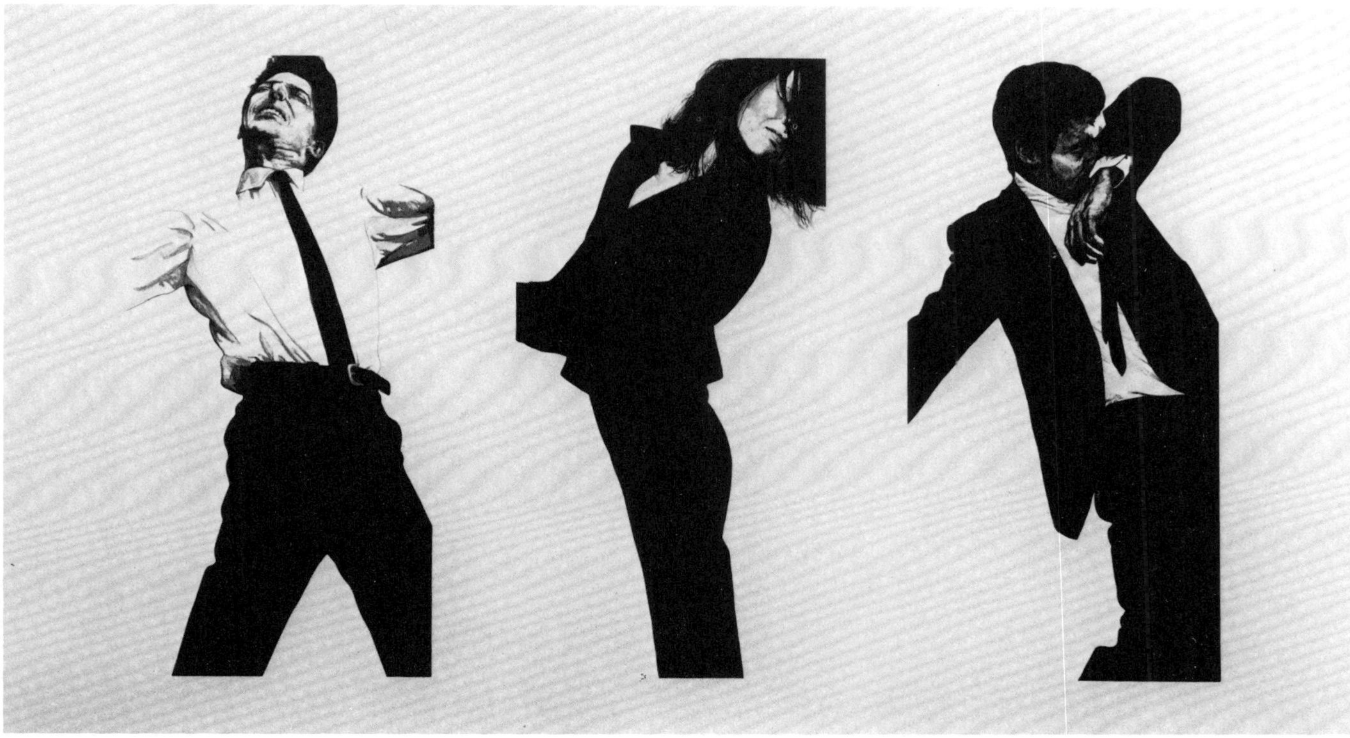

Robert Longo, *Jules, Gretchen, Mark*, 1983.

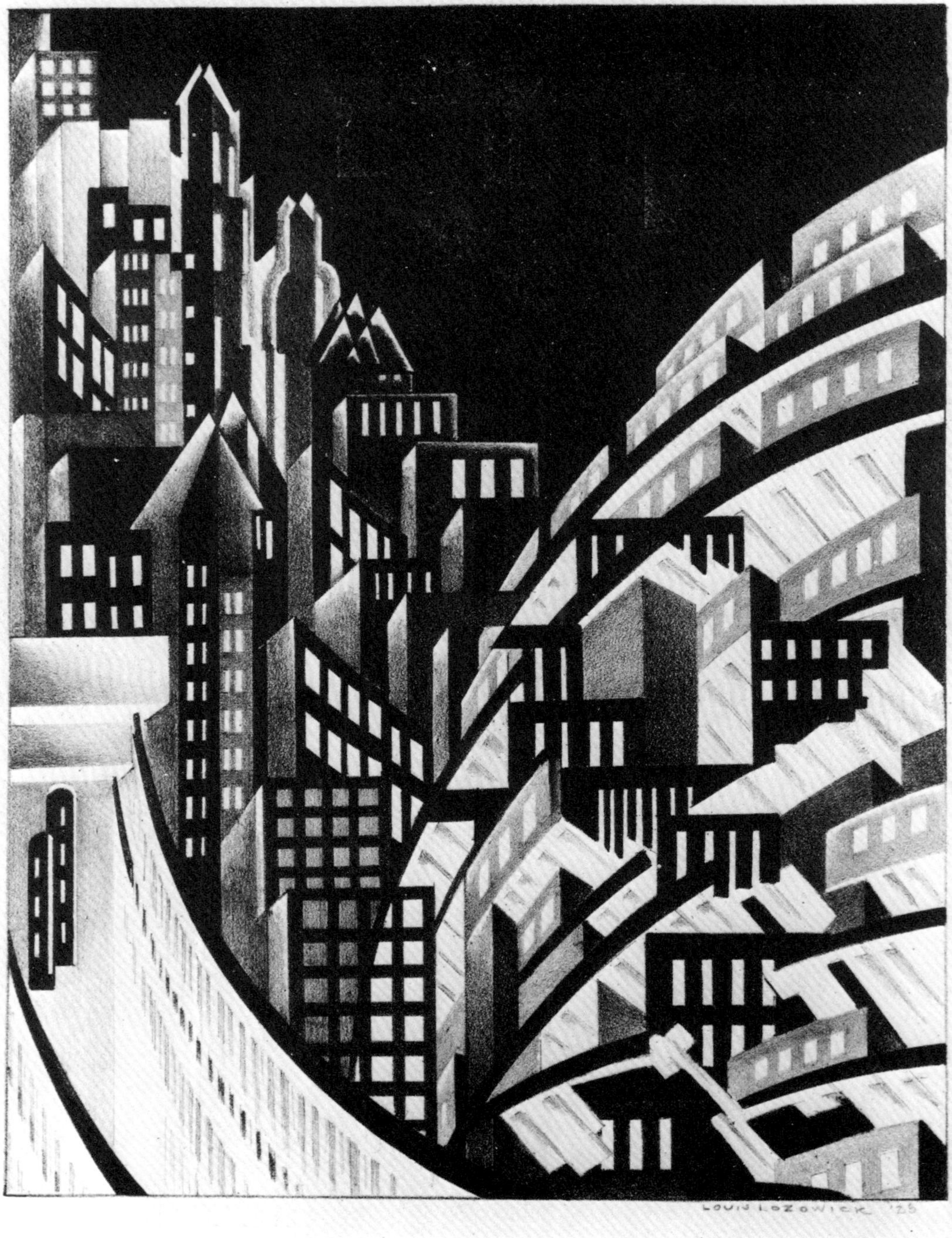

Louis Lozowick, *New York*, 1925.

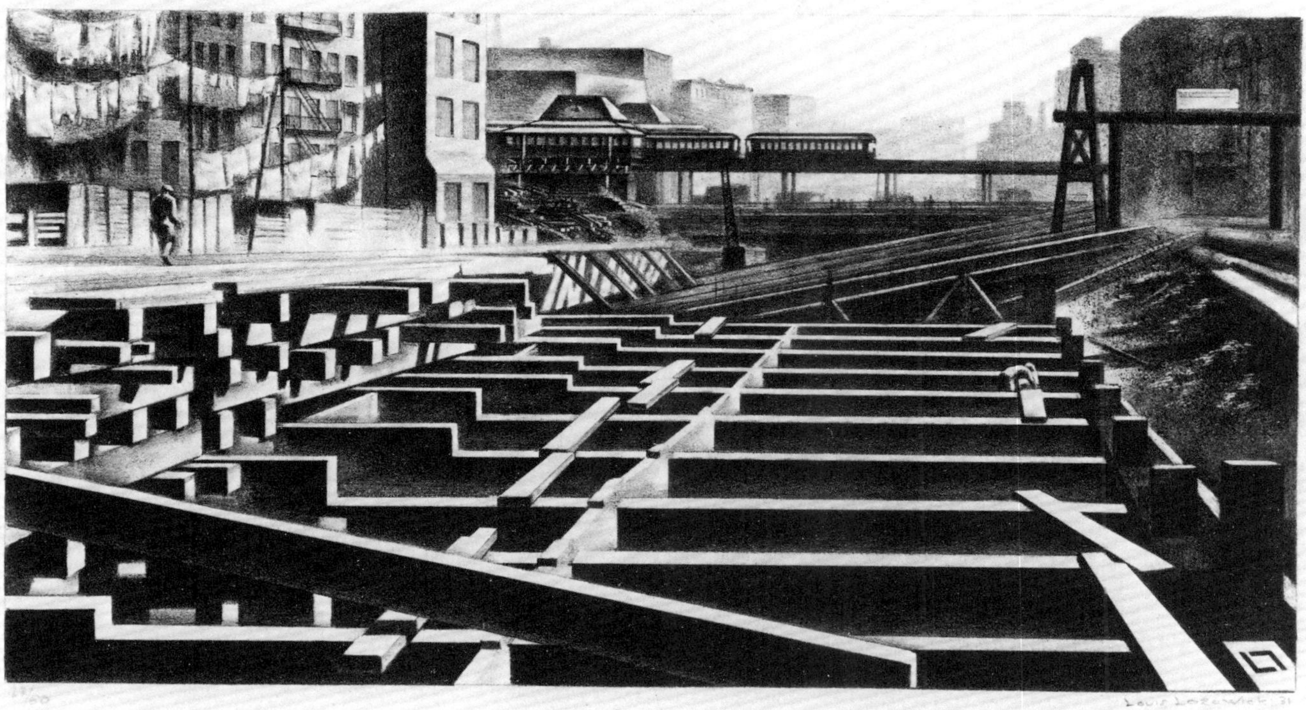

Louis Lozowick, *Subway Construction*, 1931.

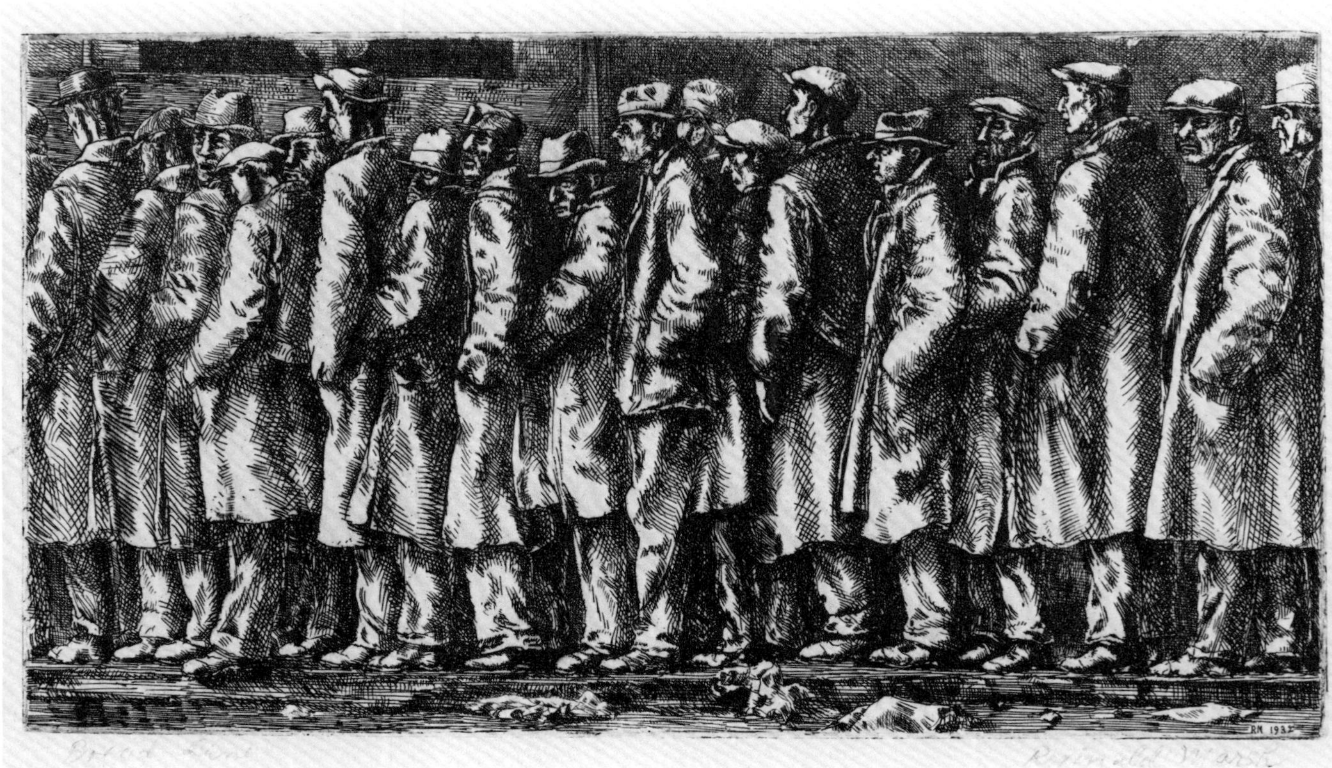

Reginald Marsh, *Bread Line—No One Has Starved*, State III, 1932.

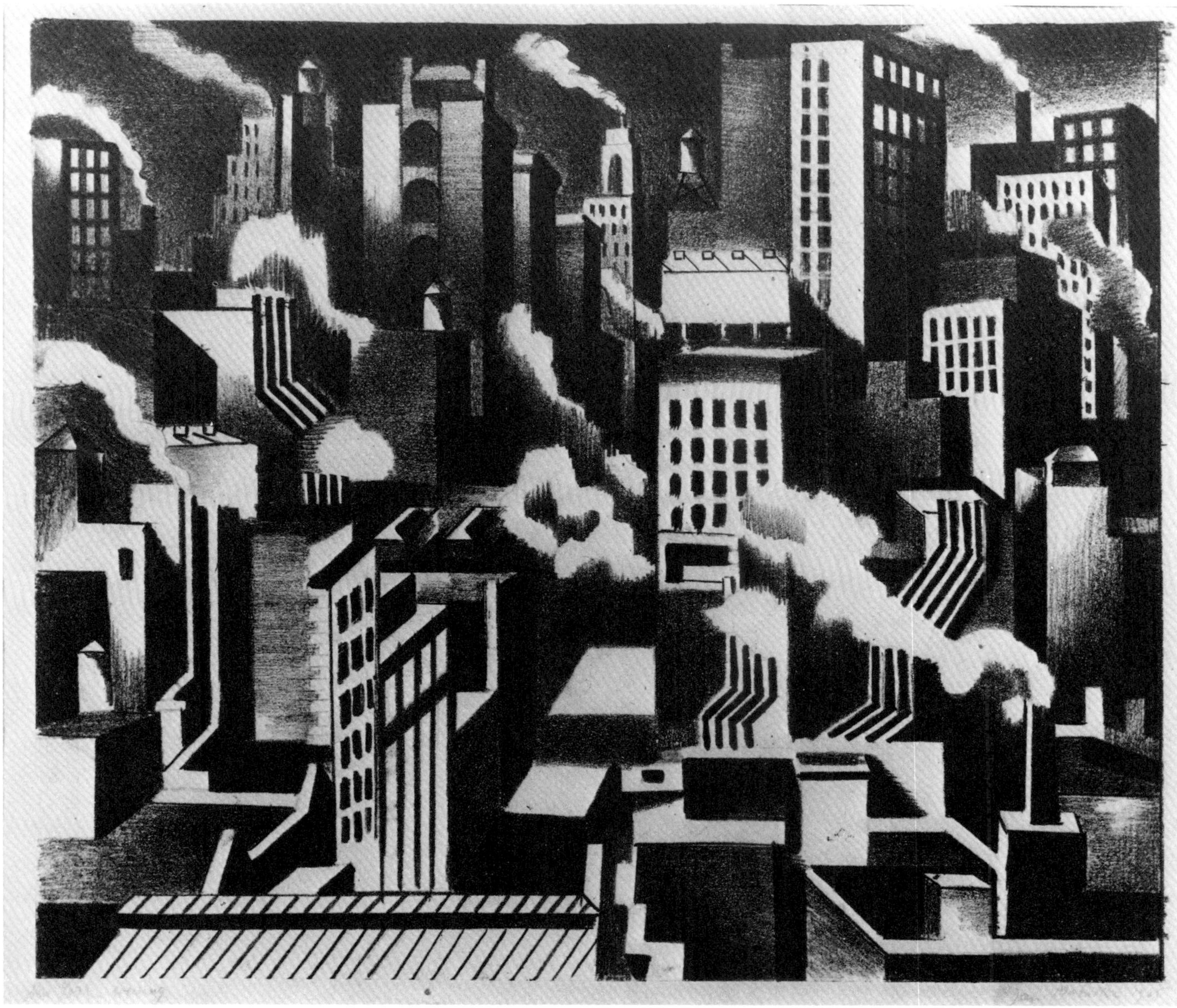

Jan Matulka, *New York Evening*, 1925.

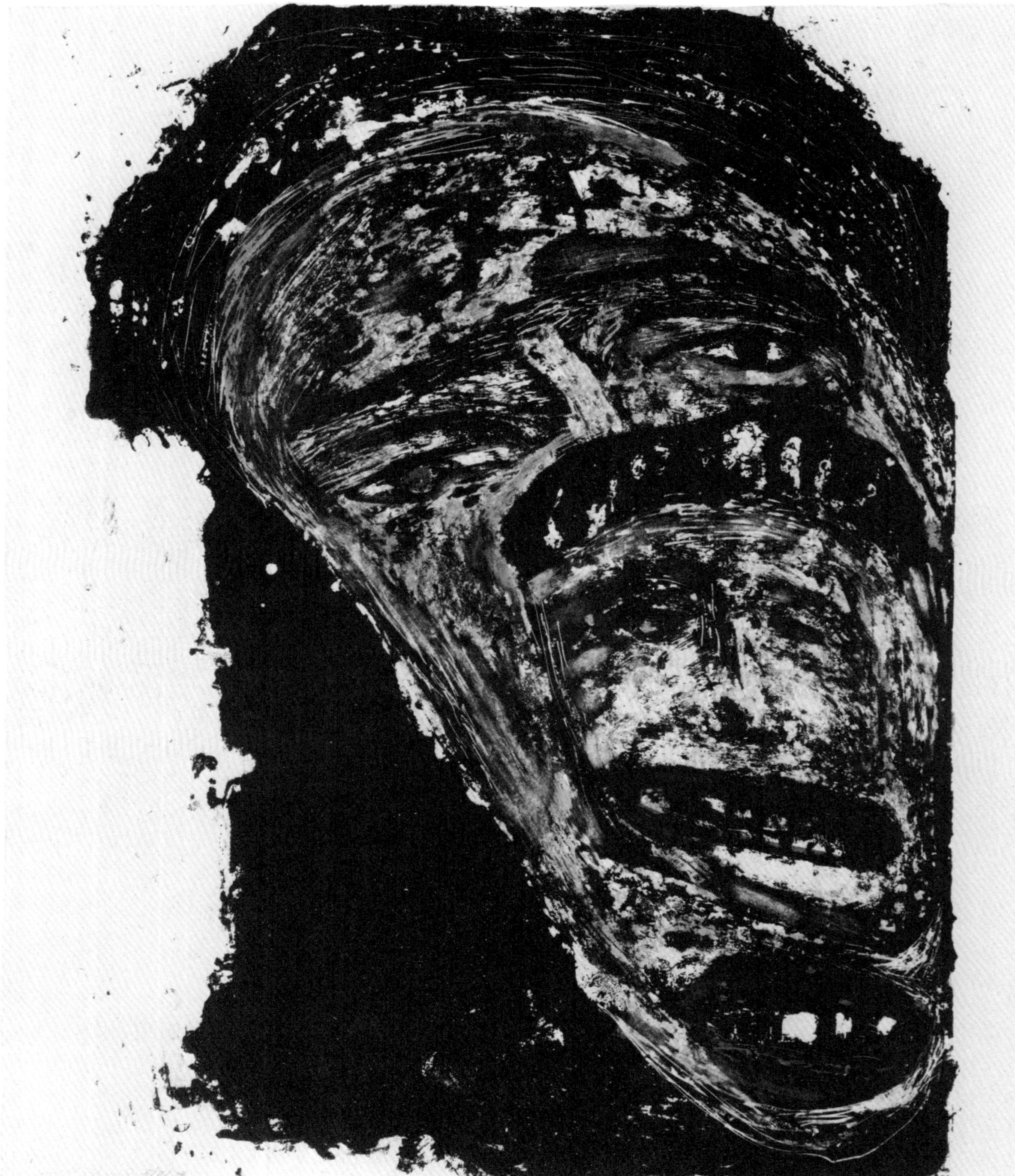

George McNeil, *Double Head #1*, 1974.

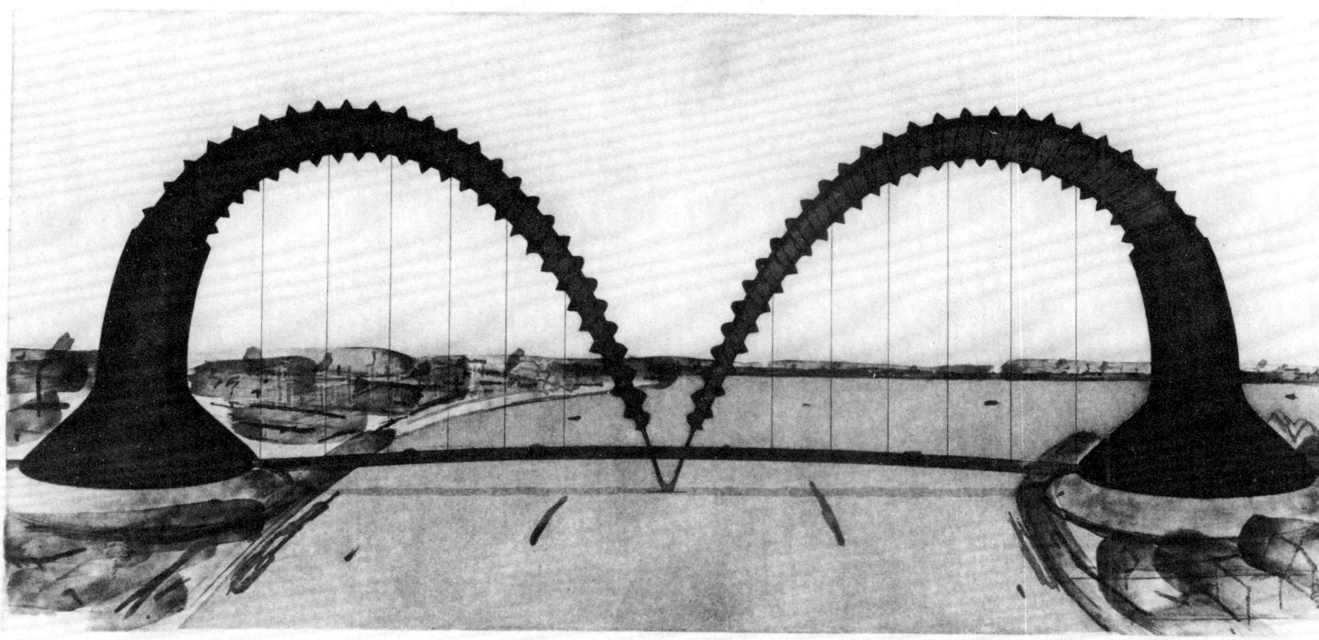

Claes Oldenburg, *Double Screwarch Bridge*, State II, Working Proof, 1981.

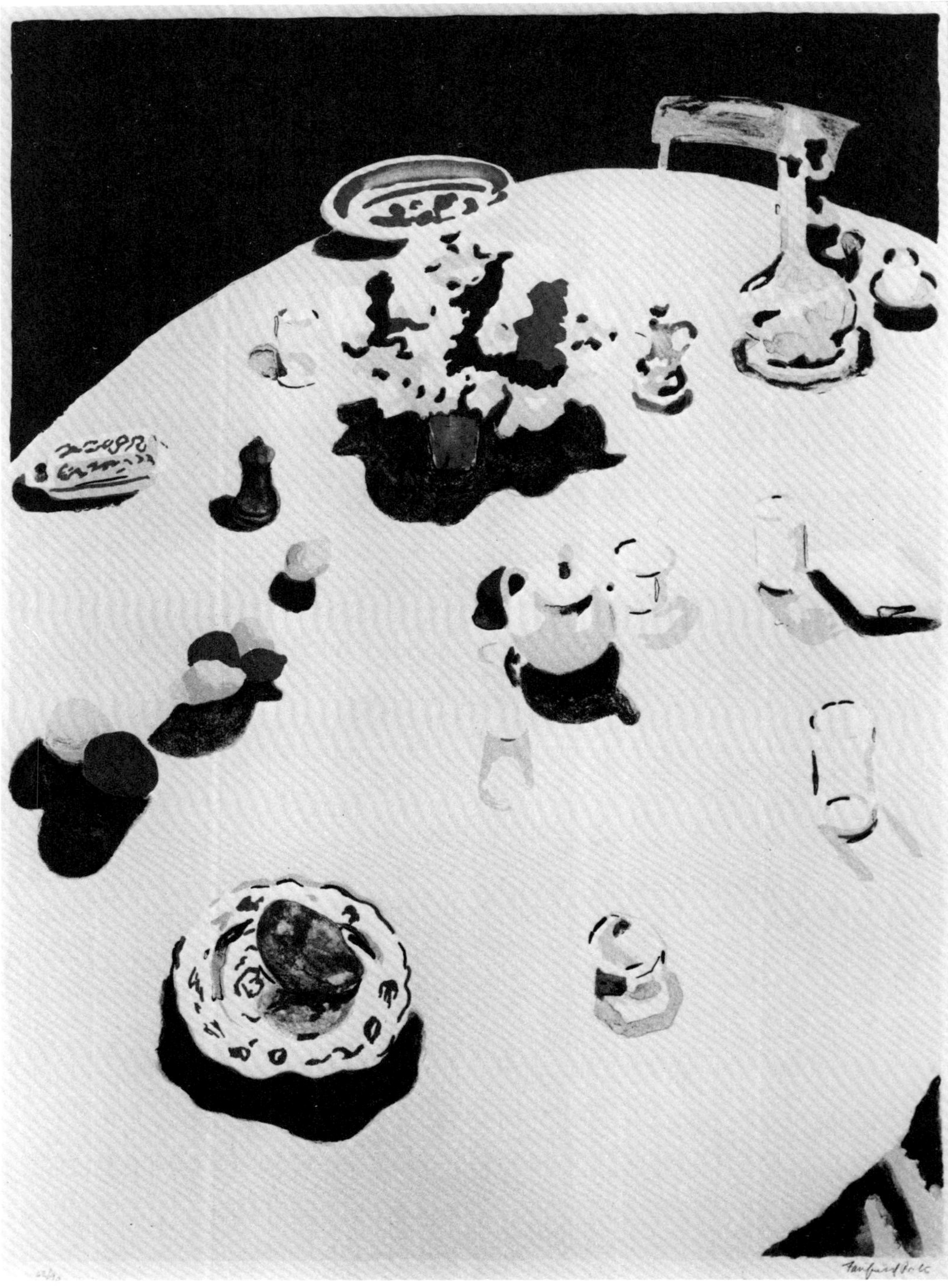

Fairfield Porter, *Table*, 1971.

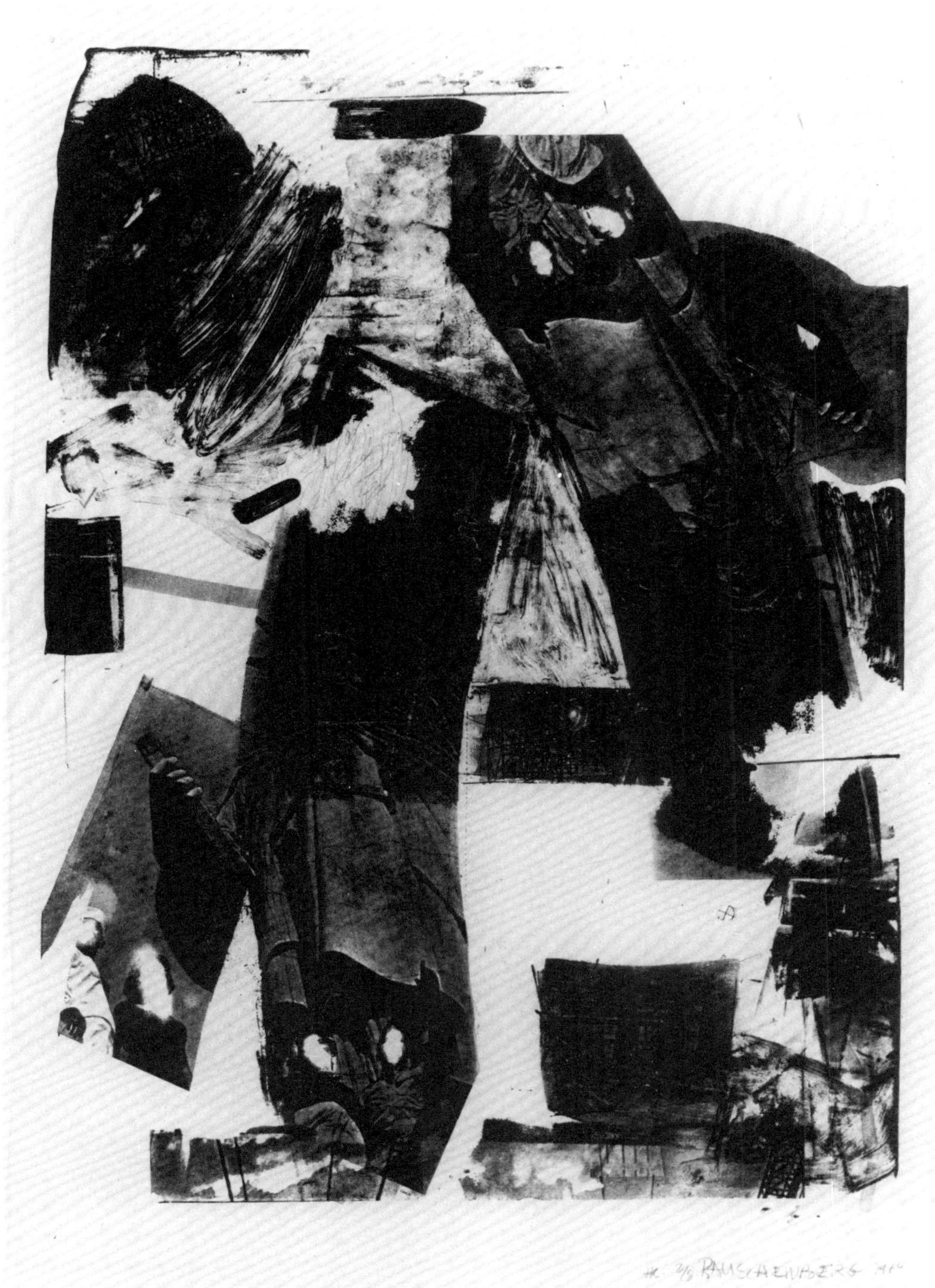

Robert Rauschenberg, *Front Roll*, 1964.

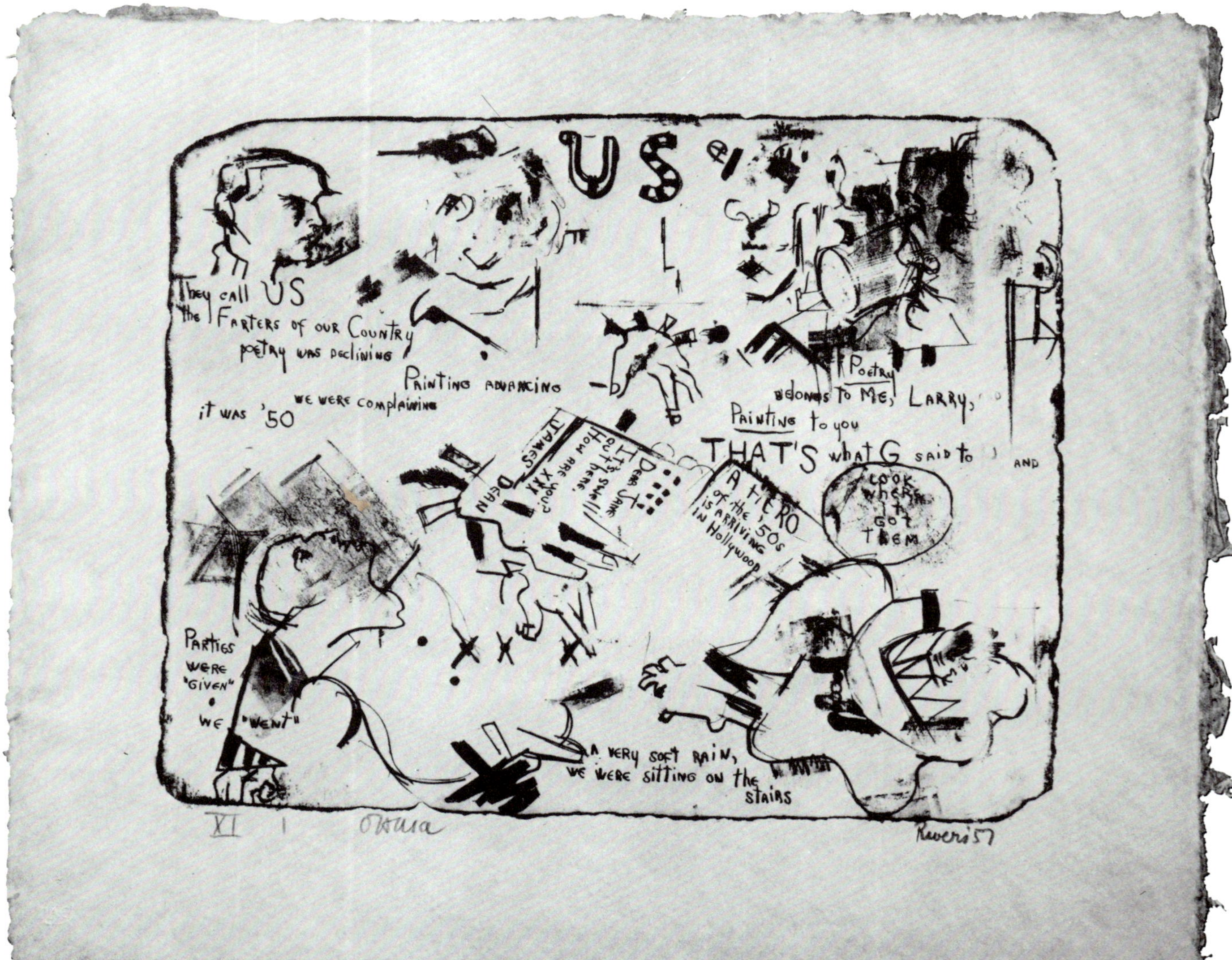

Larry Rivers with Frank O'Hara, "*US / They call US / the farters of our Country . . .* ," from the book *Stones*, 1959.

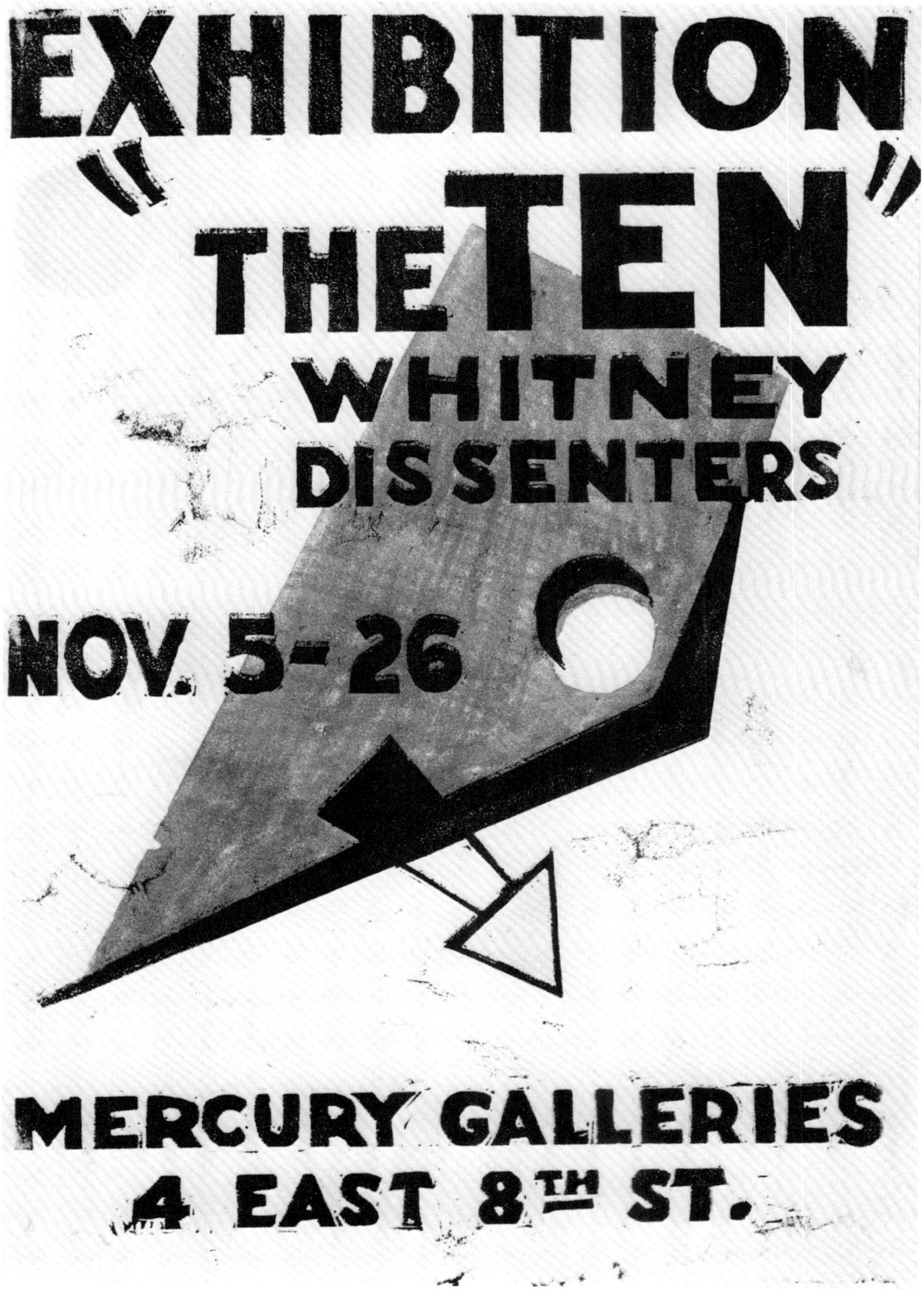

Louis Schanker, *The Ten Whitney Dissenters*, 1935.

Joel Shapiro, *Untitled*, from the series *Untitled*, 1975.

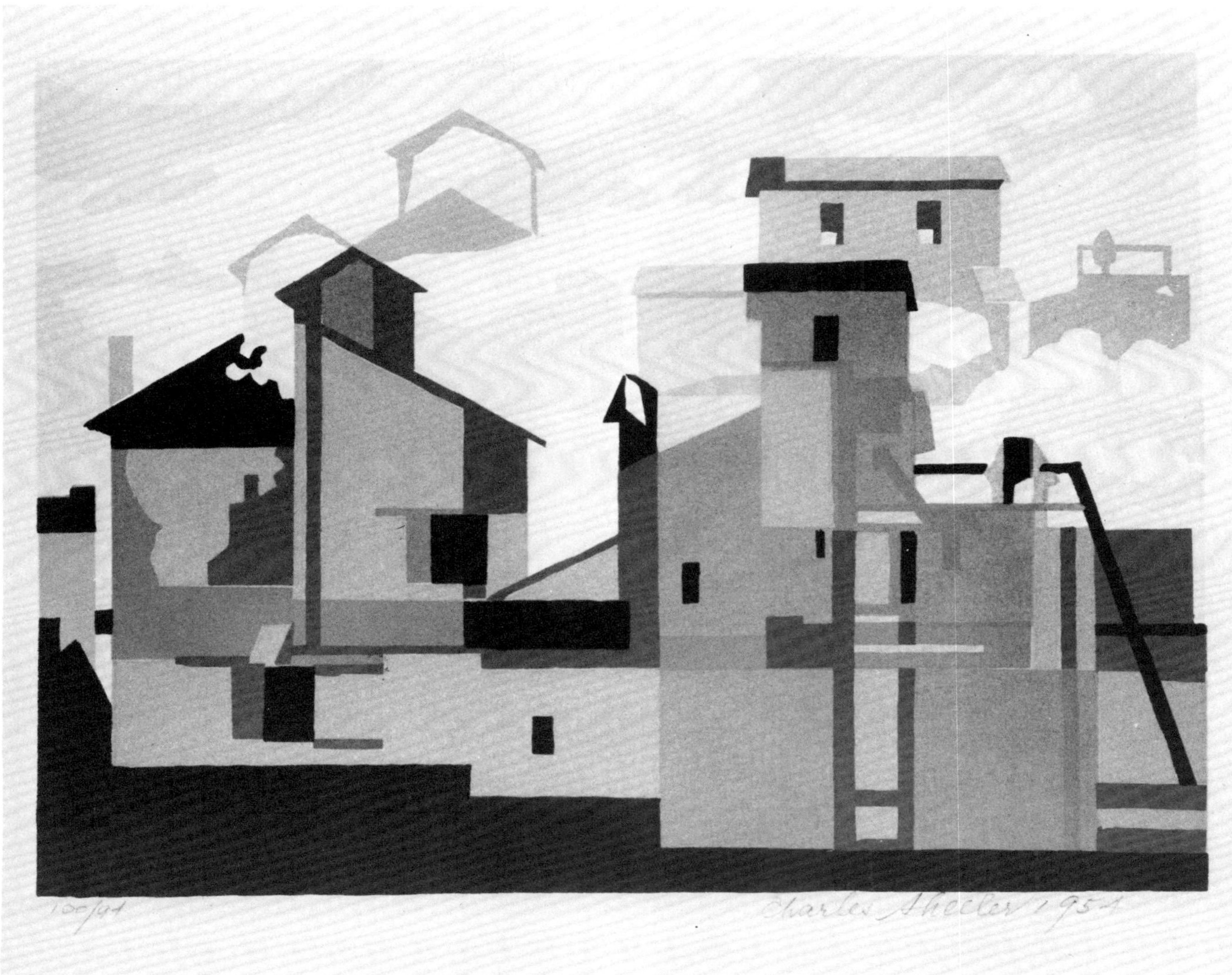

Charles Sheeler, *Architectural Cadences*, 1954.

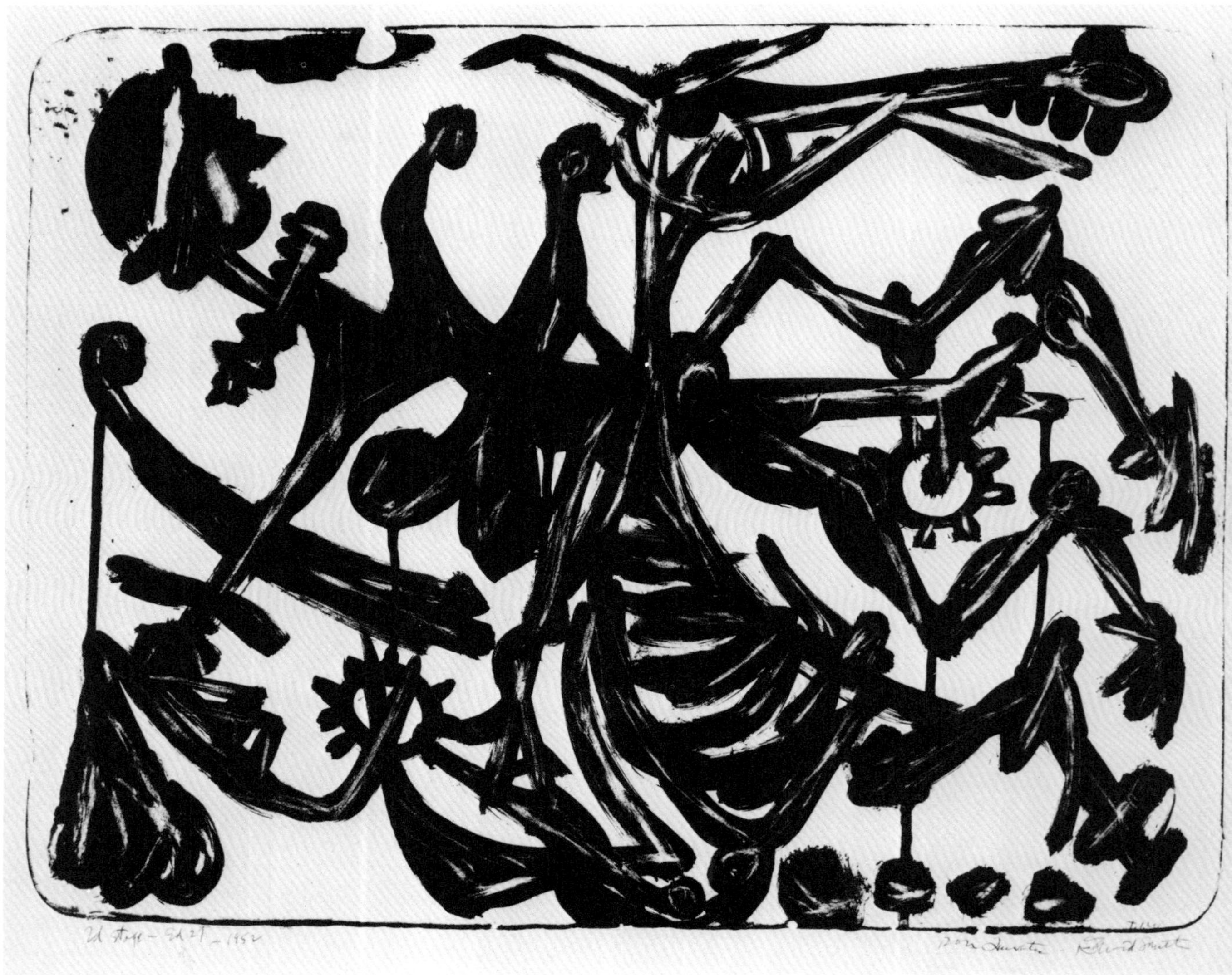

David Smith, *Don Quixote*, State II, 1952.

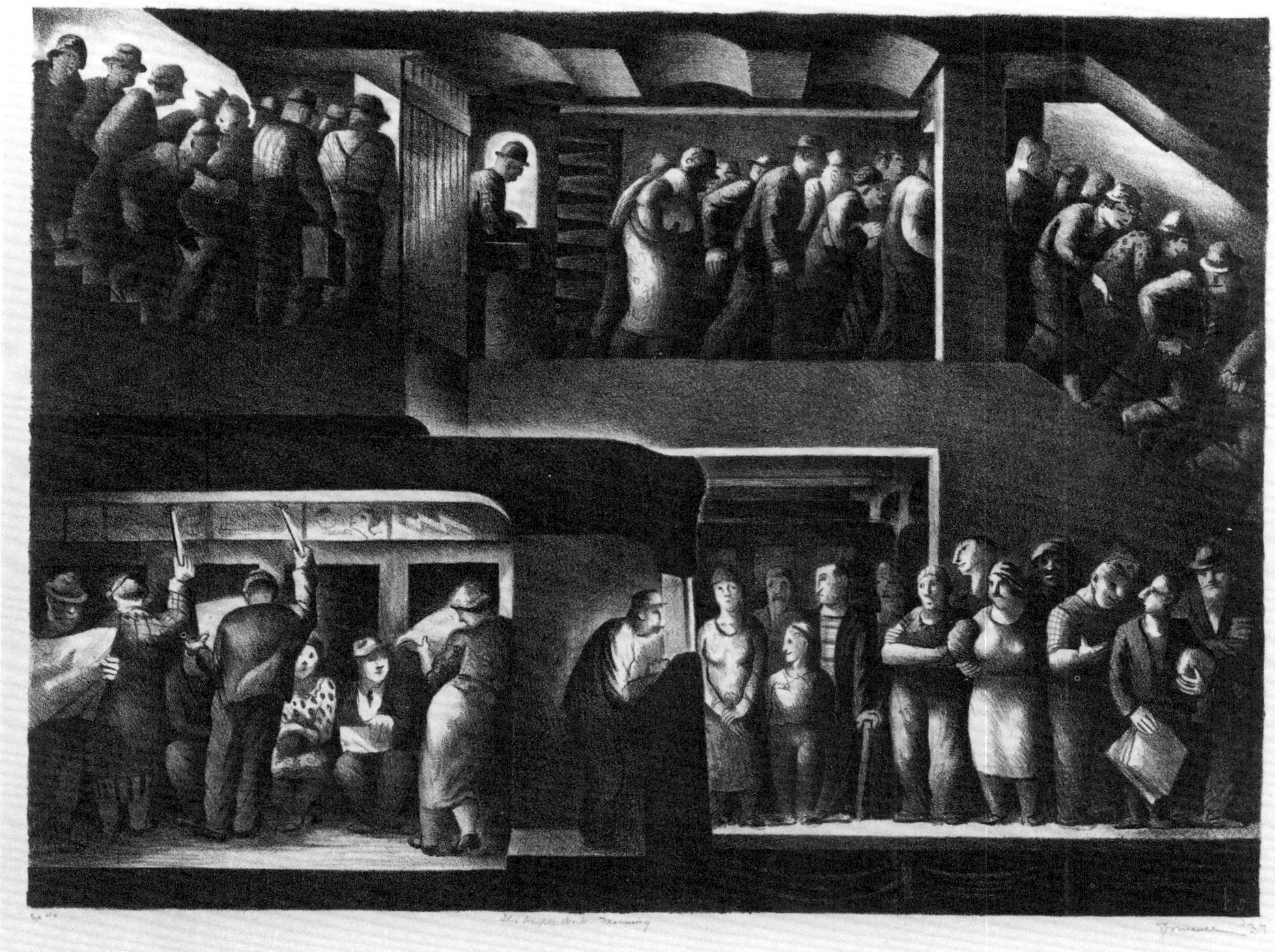

Benton Spruance, *The People Work—Morning*, 1937.

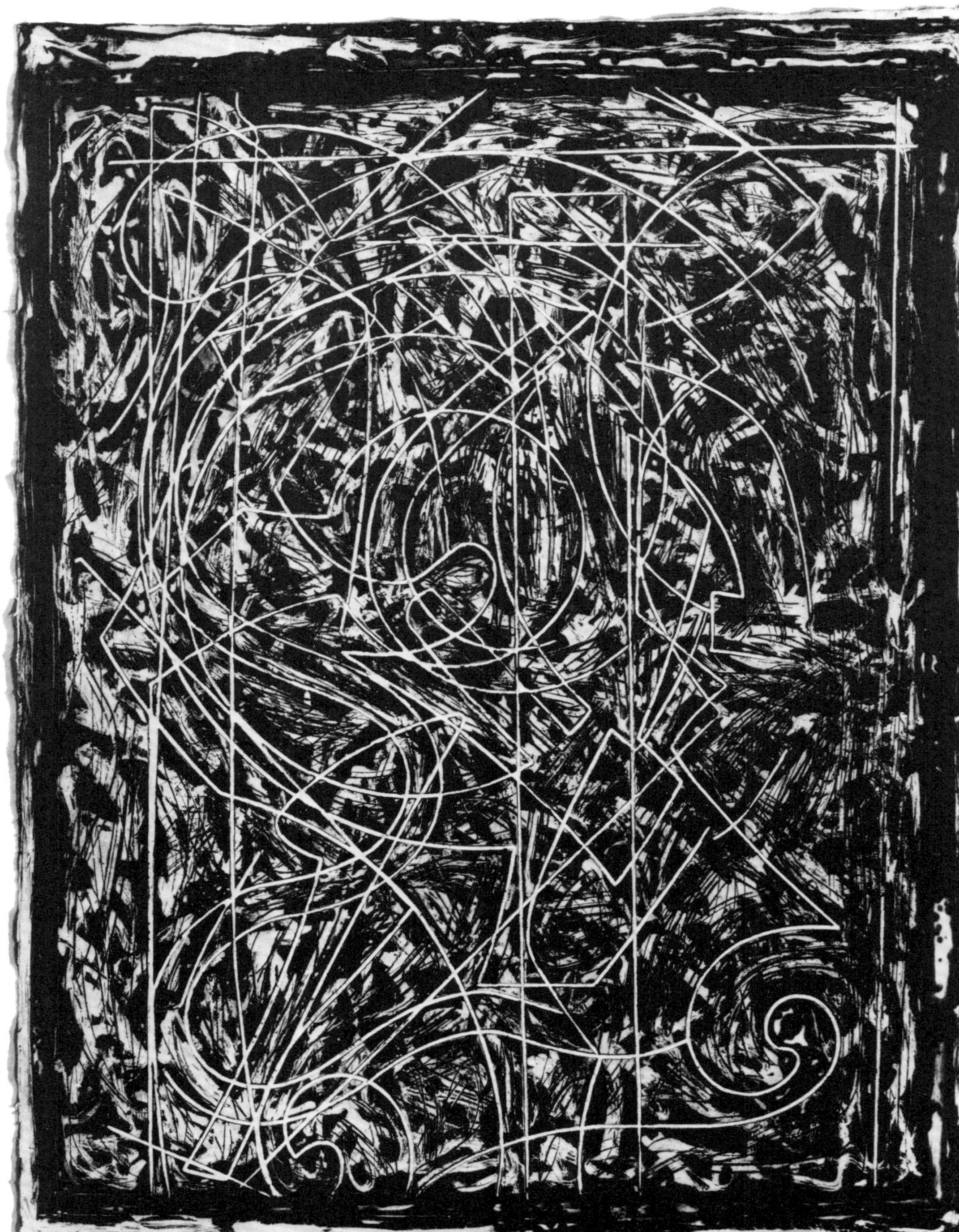

Frank Stella, *Talladega Three I*, 1982.

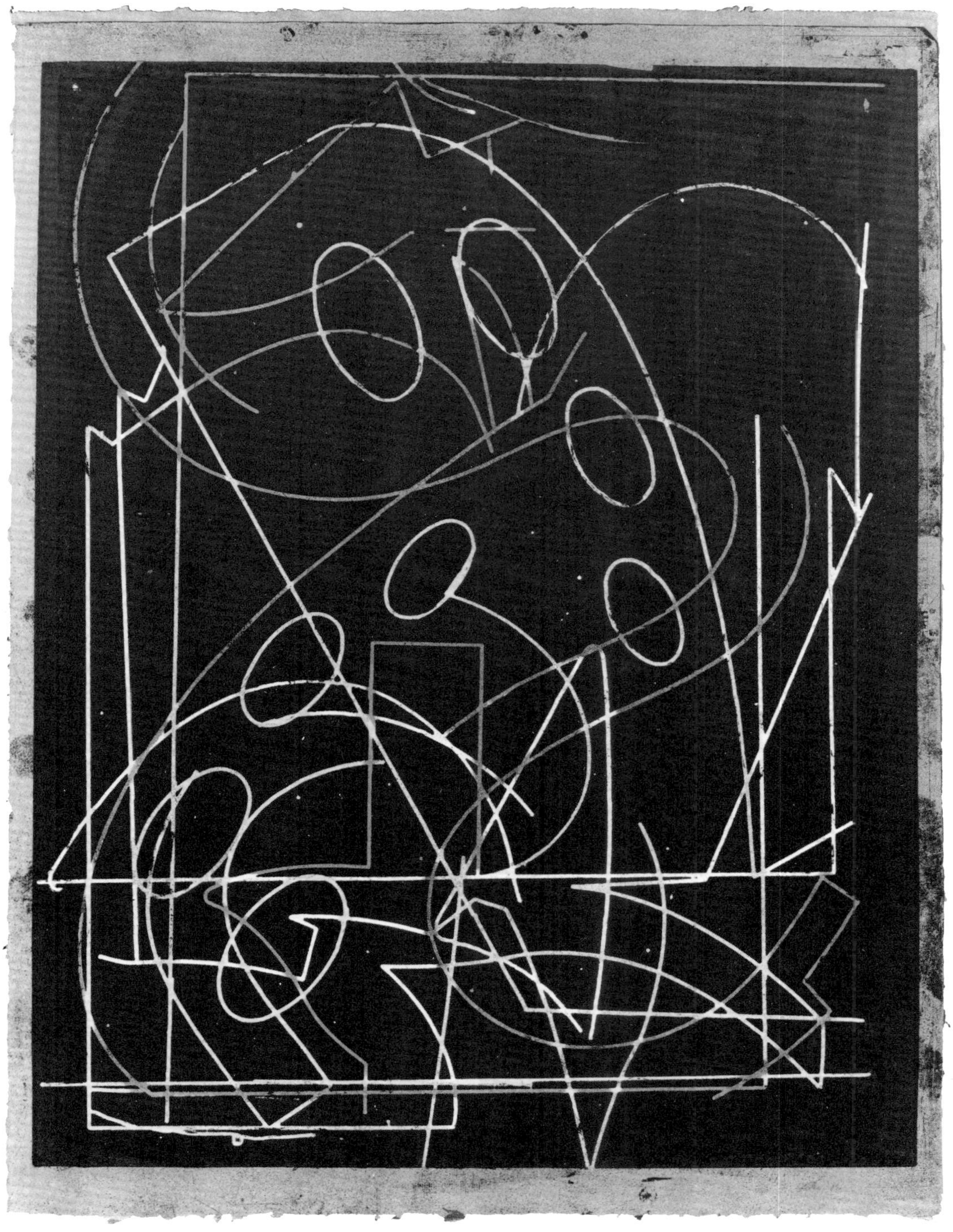

Frank Stella, *Talladega Five I*, 1982.

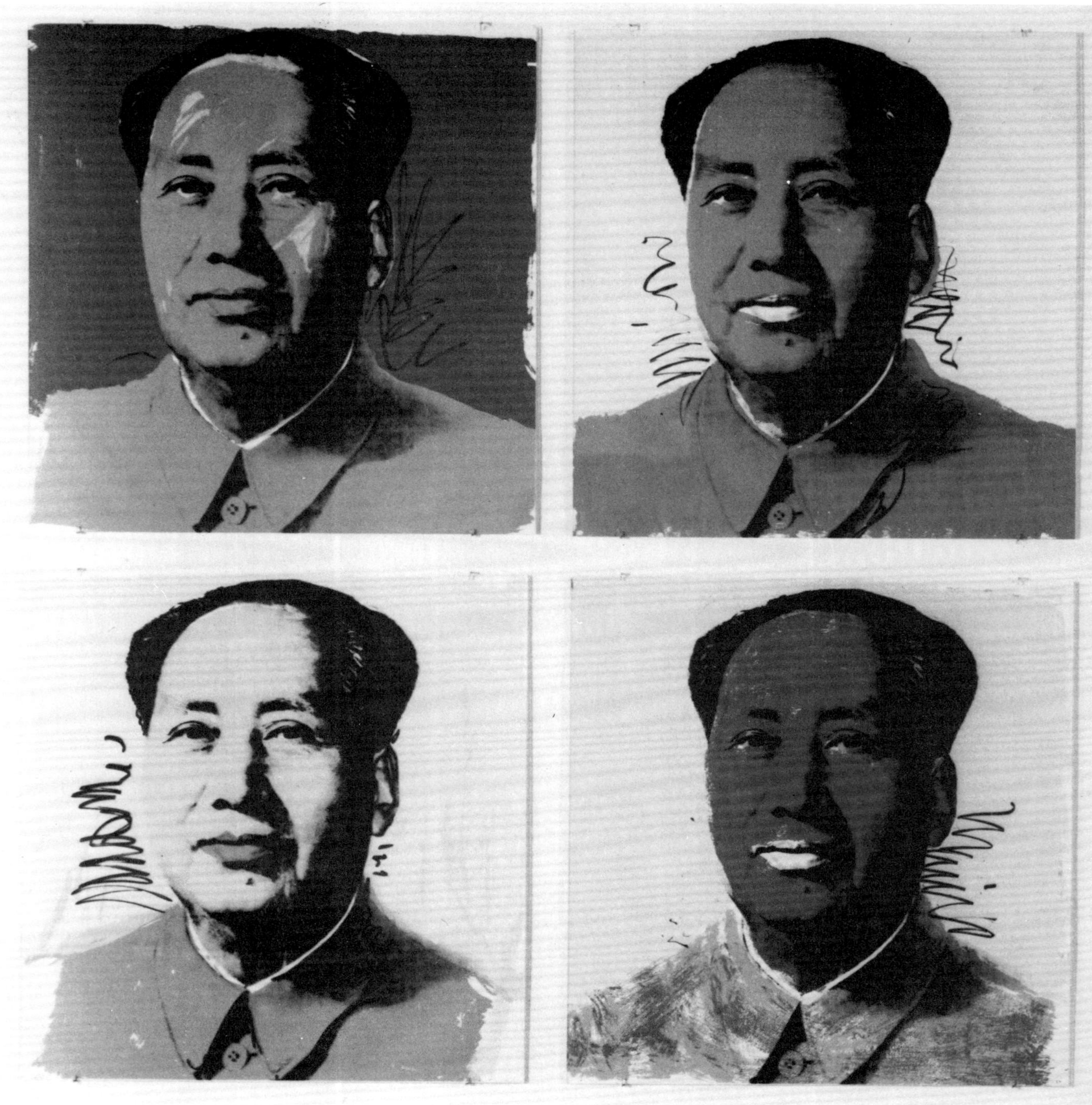

Andy Warhol, *Mao Tse-Tung*, from the portfolio *Mao Tse-Tung*, 1972.

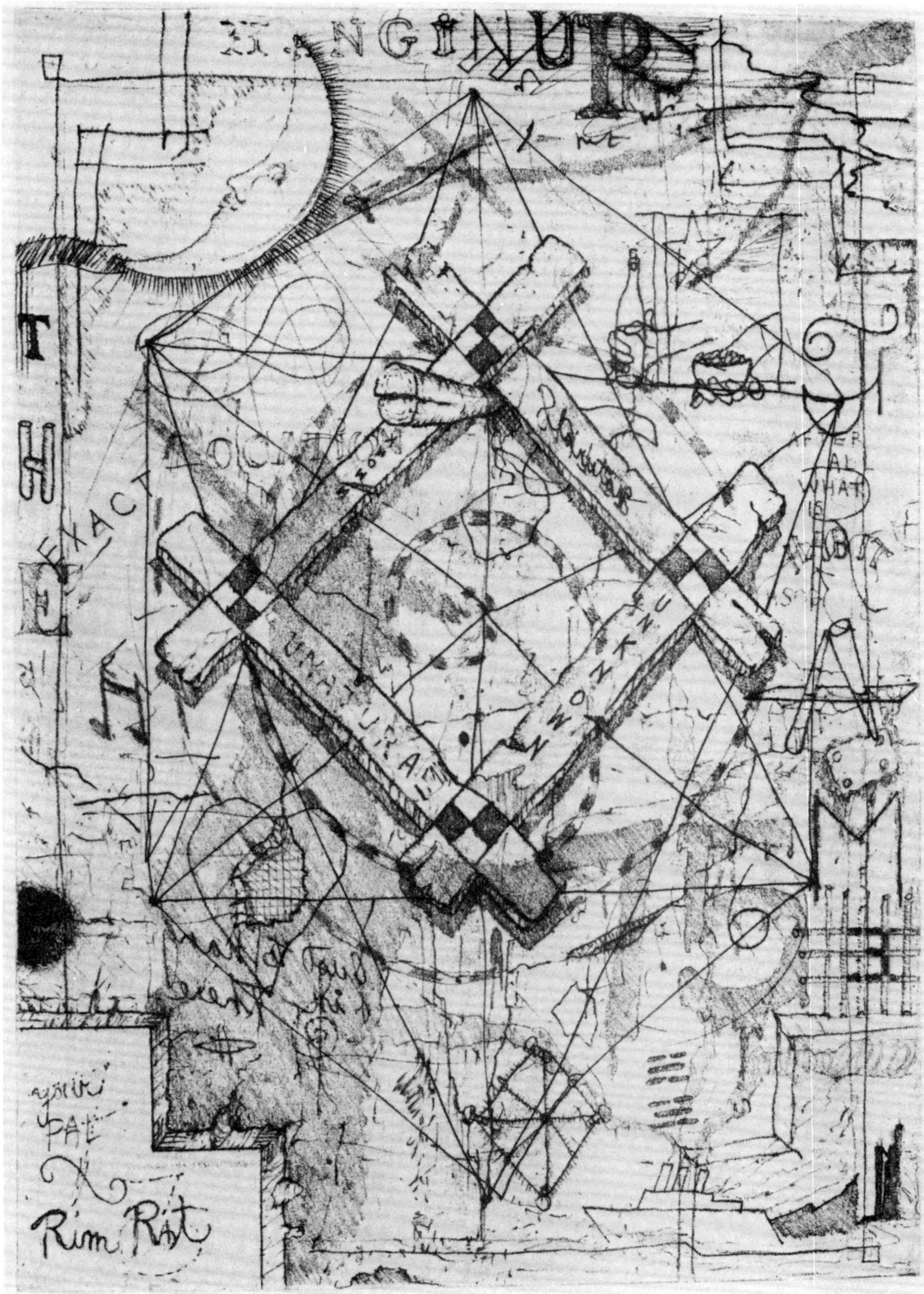

William T. Wiley, *Hanging Up the Frame*, from the book *Suite of Daze*, 1977.

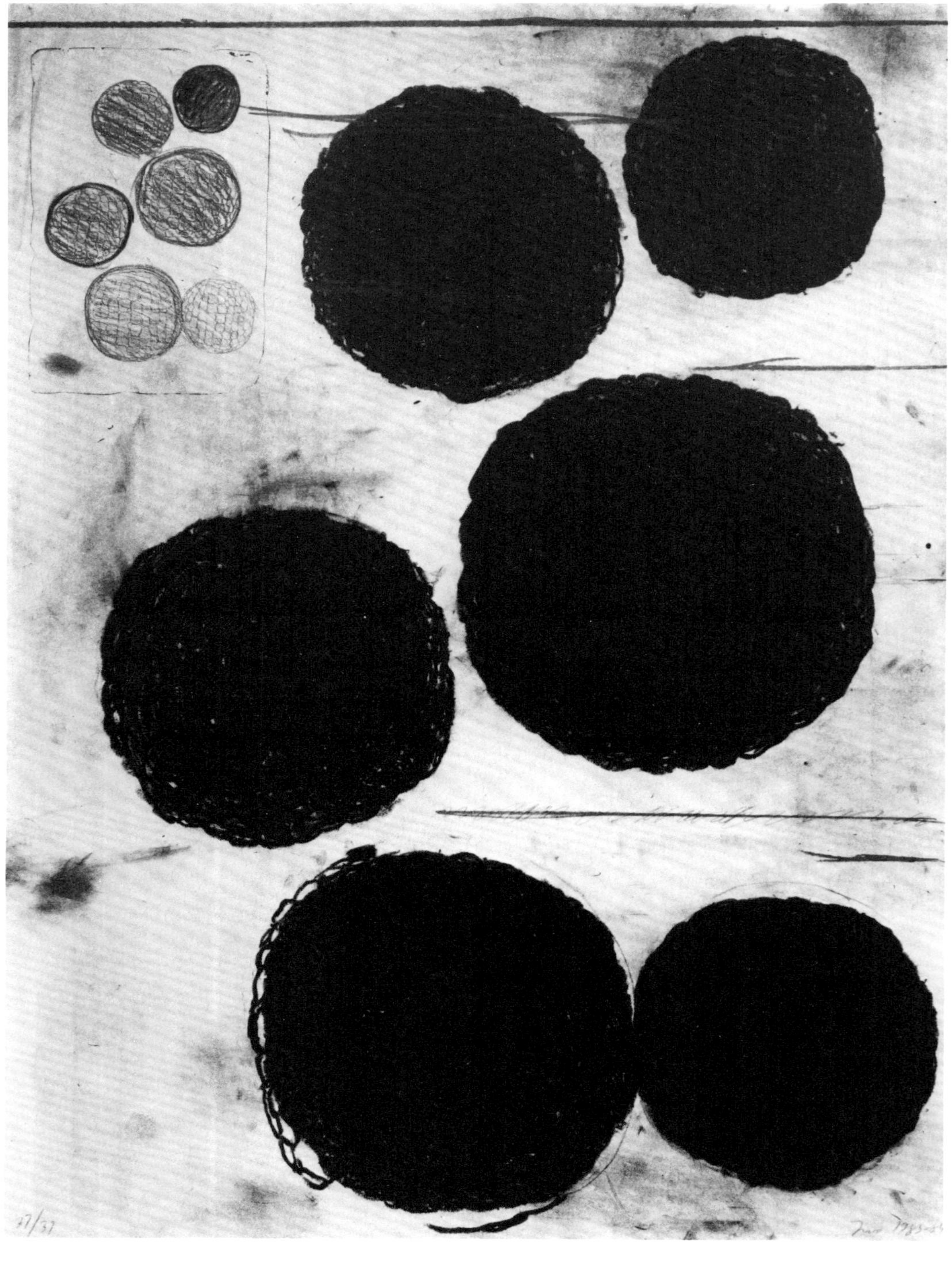

Terry Winters, *Morula II*, 1983–84.

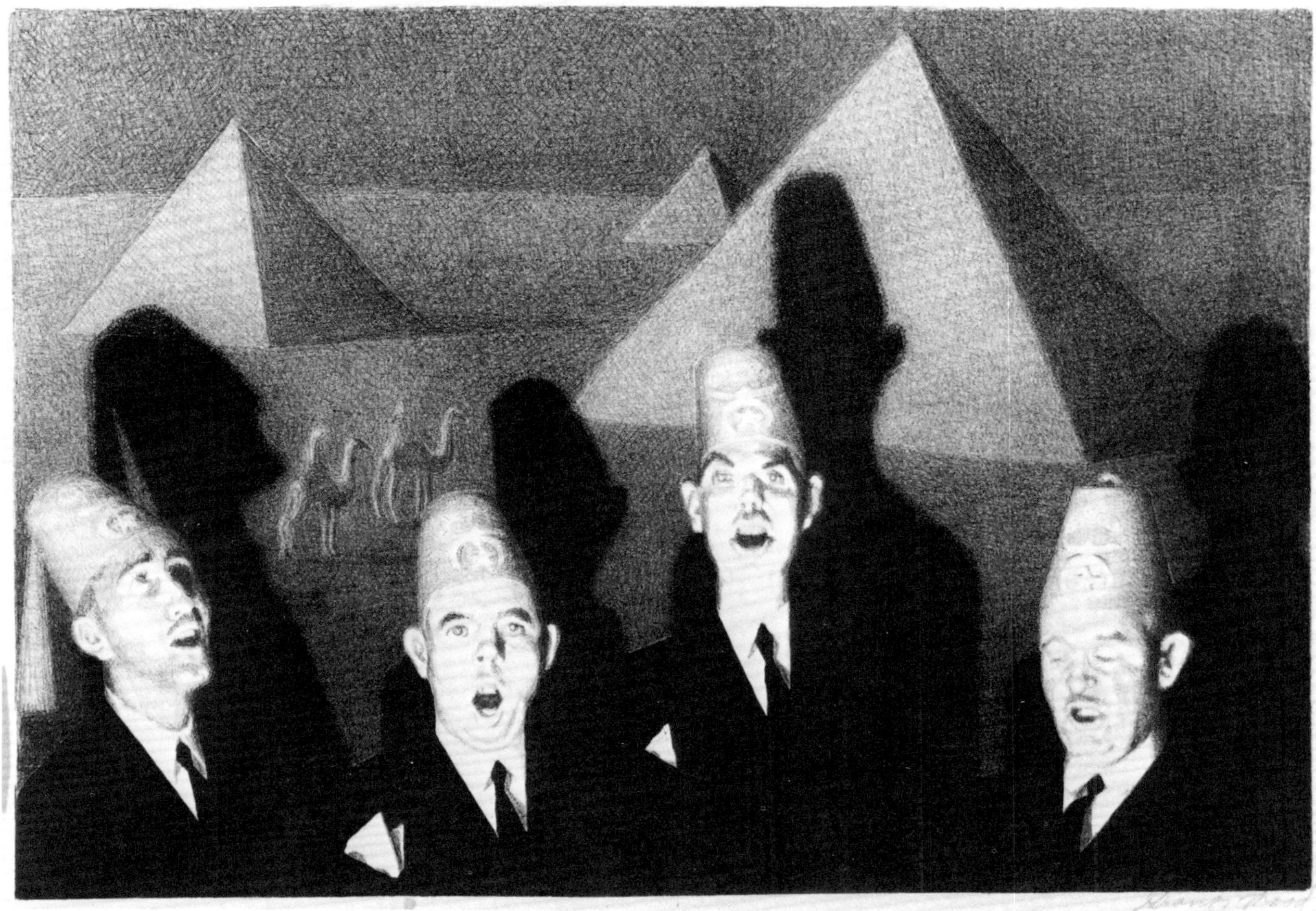

Grant Wood, *Shrine Quartet*, 1939.

Works in the Exhibition

This catalogue represents a complete listing of prints acquired by the Museum from July 1, 1973, to June 30, 1984; it constitutes a supplement to the *Catalogue of the Collection*, published in 1974.

Dimensions are in inches followed by centimeters; height precedes width. Asterisks indicate works in the exhibition.

PUBLISHERS:

Brooke Alexander, Inc., New York: Richard Artschwager, *Interior*; Jack Beal, *Self-Portrait*; Richard Bosman, *Survivor*; Alex Katz, *Face of the Poet*; Robert Longo, *Jules, Gretchen, Mark*; and Fairfield Porter, *Table*.

Crown Point Press, Oakland, California, and New York: Richard Diebenkorn, *Black Club*.

Gemini G.E.L., Los Angeles: Roy Lichtenstein, *The Reclining Nude*.

Landfall Press, Inc., Chicago and New York: William T. Wiley, *Suite of Daze*.

Multiples, Inc., New York: Jennifer Bartlett, *Day and Night I*; Claes Oldenburg, *Double Screwarch Bridge*; and Andy Warhol, *Mao Tse-Tung*.

Parasol Press, S.A., New York: Richard Estes, *Untitled*.

Skowhegan School of Painting and Sculpture, Skowhegan, Maine, and New York and Sherwood Press, New York: Philip Guston, *The Street*.

Tyler Graphics Ltd., Bedford Village, New York: Ellsworth Kelly, *Wall*; and Frank Stella, *Swan Engraving III*, *Talladega Five I*, and *Talladega Three I*.

Universal Limited Art Editions, West Islip, New York: Helen Frankenthaler, *Lot's Wife*; Fritz Glarner, *Recollection*; Jasper Johns, *Savarin* (1977–81), *Savarin* (1978), *Souvenir*, and *Untitled*; Robert Rauschenberg, *Front Roll*; Larry Rivers with Frank O'Hara, *Stones*; and Terry Winters, *Morula II*.

Josef Albers (1888–1976)

Ascension, from the series *Graphic Tectonics*, 1942
Lithograph: sheet, 23¾ x 19 (60.3 x 48.3);
image, 17¼ x 8³⁄₁₆ (43.8 x 20.8)
Purchase, with funds from Philip Morris Incorporated 74.85*

Intaglio Solo XIII, 1962
Embossed print: sheet, 14 x 20⅜ (35.6 x 51.8);
image, 7¹¹⁄₁₆ x 10¼ (19.5 x 26)
Gift of Mr. and Mrs. Sylvan Cole, Jr. 81.35.1*

Ivan Le Lorraine Albright (1897–1983)

Show Case Doll, 1954
Lithograph: sheet, 20⅛ x 27⅞ (51.1 x 70.8);
image, 17⅜ x 25½ (44.1 x 64.8)
Gift of an Anonymous Donor 73.44*

Gregory Amenoff (b. 1948)

In the Fifth Season, 1983
Woodcut: sheet, 40¾ x 36½ (103.5 x 92.7);
image, 36⅛ x 31⅞ (91.8 x 81)
Gift of Mr. and Mrs. Thomas H. Dittmer 84.24*

John Taylor Arms (1887–1953)

Castles in the Air, 1921
Lithograph: sheet, 17½ x 12¾ (44.5 x 32.4);
image, 15½ x 10⅜ (39.4 x 26.3)
Gift of Aldis Browne Fine Arts, Ltd. 74.86

Richard Artschwager (b. 1924)

Interior, 1972
Screenprint: sheet and image, 32¾ x 46 (83.2 x 116.8)
Purchase, with funds from the Neysa McMein Purchase Award 79.44*

George C. Ault (1891–1948)

Came's House, 1934
Lithograph: sheet, 16 x 11⅜ (40.6 x 29.9);
image, 14 x 10 (35.6 x 25.4)
Gift of an Anonymous Donor 77.95*

Milton Avery (1885–1965)

Rothko with Pipe, Trial Proof, 1936
Drypoint: sheet, 11½ x 10 (29.2 x 25.4);
image, 7⅛ x 6⅞ (18.1 x 17.4)
Purchase, with funds from the Print Committee 83.24*

Rosalie, 1939
Drypoint: sheet, 11⅞ x 10 (30.2 x 25.4);
image, 6⁷⁄₁₆ x 4½ (16.4 x 11.4)
Gift of Ruth and Richard Shack 83.53*

Dancer, Artist's Proof, 1954
Woodcut: sheet, 17½ x 12 (44.5 x 30.5);
image, 12 x 9 (30.5 x 24.4)
Gift of Mr. and Mrs. Dave H. Williams 82.47.1*

Birds and Sea, Trial Proof, 1955
Woodcut: sheet, 11⅞ x 27⅝ (30.2 x 70.2);
image, 9¾ x 24 (24.8 x 61)
Purchase, with funds from the Print Committee 83.46*

Gray Sea, 1963
Lithograph: sheet, 22¹⁵⁄₁₆ x 28⁵⁄₁₆ (58.3 x 71.9); image, 21¼ x 26½ (54 x 67.3)
Gift of Mr. and Mrs. Sylvan Cole, Jr. 81.35.2*

Peggy Bacon (b. 1895)

Lunch No. 4—Custard (*Custard*), 1928
Lithograph: sheet, 11¼ x 16 (28.6 x 40.6);
image, 5½ x 11 (14 x 27.9)
Bequest of Felicia Meyer Marsh 80.31.115

John Baeder (b. 1938)

Empire Diner, 1976
Mezzotint: sheet, 17$\frac{3}{4}$ x 24$\frac{13}{16}$ (45.1 x 63); image, 8$\frac{3}{4}$ x 13$\frac{11}{16}$ (22.2 x 34.8)
Gift of Richard Steinberg 77.16*

Jo Baer (b. 1929)

Cardinations, No. 7, from the portfolio *Cardinations*, 1974
Screenprint: sheet, 28$\frac{1}{2}$ x 21 (72.4 x 53.3); image, 24$\frac{7}{16}$ x 18$\frac{1}{2}$ (62.1 x 47)
Purchase, with funds from the Frederic M. Chacker Fund 74.87

William Bailey (b. 1930)

Still Life No. 6, State I, 1982
Lithograph: sheet, 24$\frac{5}{8}$ x 20$\frac{5}{8}$ (62.5 x 52.4); image, 18$\frac{1}{8}$ x 14$\frac{1}{8}$ (46.1 x 35.9)
Purchase, with funds from Barbara Babcock Millhouse 82.28*

Will Barnet (b. 1911)

Woman & White Cat, 1971
Screenprint: sheet, 25$\frac{1}{2}$ x 21$\frac{1}{2}$ (64.8 x 54.6); image, 23$\frac{1}{2}$ x 20 (59 x 50.8)
Gift of the Circle Gallery, Ltd. 73.52

Jennifer Bartlett (b. 1941)

Day and Night I, 1978
Drypoint: sheet and image, 30$\frac{3}{4}$ x 20$\frac{5}{16}$ (78.1 x 51.6)
Purchase, with funds from Mr. and Mrs. Frederic M. Roberts in memory of their son James Reed Roberts 79.34.3*

Day and Night II, 1978
Drypoint: sheet and image, 31$\frac{1}{8}$ x 21 (79.1 x 53.3)
Purchase, with funds from Mr. and Mrs. Frederic M. Roberts in memory of their son James Reed Roberts 79.34.2*

Day and Night III, 1978
Drypoint: sheet and image, 31 x 21 (78.7 x 53.3)
Purchase, with funds from Mr. and Mrs. Frederic M. Roberts in memory of their son James Reed Roberts 79.34.1*

Jack Beal (b. 1931)

Self-Portrait, 1974–75
Lithograph: sheet, 30$\frac{1}{16}$ x 22$\frac{3}{8}$ (76.4 x 56.8); image, 27 x 20$\frac{1}{2}$ (68.6 x 52.1)
Purchase, with funds from the Print Committee 83.12*

George Bellows (1882–1925)

Benediction in Georgia, 1916
Lithograph: sheet, 21$\frac{1}{8}$ x 26$\frac{1}{4}$ (53.6 x 66.7); image, 16$\frac{1}{4}$ x 20 (41.3 x 50.8)
Purchase, with funds from the Print Committee 83.14*

Splinter Beach, 1916
Lithograph: sheet, 16$\frac{1}{2}$ x 21 (41.9 x 53.3); image, 15 x 19$\frac{7}{8}$ (38.1 x 50.5)
Purchase 73.69*

Sixteen East Gay Street, 1924
Lithograph: sheet, 11$\frac{3}{8}$ x 13$\frac{1}{2}$ (28.9 x 34.3); image, 9$\frac{7}{16}$ x 11$\frac{3}{4}$ (24 x 29.8)
Gift of Mr. and Mrs. Samuel L. Rosenfeld 77.105

Rosalind Bengelsdorf (1916–1979)

Untitled, from the portfolio *American Abstract Artists*, 1937
Offset lithograph: sheet, 9¼ x 12 (23.5 x 30.5); image, 7⅛ x 9⅝ (18.1 x 24.5)
Gift of Mr. and Mrs. Wolf Kahn in honor of Alice Mason 77.121.1

Thomas Hart Benton (1889–1975)

Prodigal Son, 1939
Lithograph: sheet, 12⅜ x 16⅞ (31.4 x 42.9); image, 10⅛ x 13³⁄₁₆ (25.7 x 33.5)
Gift of Arthur G. Altschul 78.24*

Charles Biederman (b. 1906)

Study for Color Sculpture Outdoors, New York, 1937
Lithograph: sheet, 24⅞ x 19 (63.2 x 48.2); image, 14⅝ x 11 (37.1 x 27.9)
Purchase, with funds from the Equitable Life Assurance Society of the United States Purchase Fund 84.14*

Study for Color Sculpture Outdoors, New York, 1937
Lithograph: sheet, 22⅞ x 15⅞ (58.1 x 40.3); image, 14¾ x 10⅞ (37.5 x 27.6)
Purchase, with funds from the Equitable Life Assurance Society of the United States Purchase Fund 84.15*

Henry Billings (b. 1901)

Machines and Men, from the series *Machines and Men*, 1931
Lithograph: sheet, 17 x 19³⁄₁₆ (43.2 x 48.7); image, 14 x 15¹³⁄₁₆ (35.6 x 40.1)
Purchase, with funds from the Print Purchase Fund 79.61*

Machines and Men, from the series *Machines and Men*, 1931
Lithograph: sheet, 15 x 19½ (38.1 x 49.5); image, 13⅜ x 15¹³⁄₁₆ (34.6 x 40.1)
Purchase, with funds from the Print Purchase Fund 79.62*

Machines and Men, from the series *Machines and Men*, 1931
Lithograph: sheet, 18½ x 16⅞ (47 x 42.9); image, 15¾ x 13¾ (40 x 34.9)
Purchase, with funds from the Print Purchase Fund 79.63*

Machines and Men, from the series *Machines and Men*, 1931
Lithograph: sheet, 19¼ x 16¾ (48.9 x 42.5); image, 15¾ x 13¾ (40 x 34.9)
Purchase, with funds from the Print Purchase Fund 79.64*

Machines and Men, from the series *Machines and Men*, 1931
Lithograph: sheet, 19¹¹⁄₁₆ x 15¹⁵⁄₁₆ (48.4 x 40.5); image, 14⅞ x 13⅛ (37.8 x 33.3)
Purchase, with funds from the Print Purchase Fund 79.65*

Isabel Bishop (b. 1902)

At the Base of the Flagpole (Idle Conversation), 1928
Etching: sheet, 7⅝ x 10⅝ (19.4 x 27); image, 5 x 6 (12.8 x 15.2)
Bequest of Felicia Meyer Marsh 80.31.120*

A Youth (Tough) 1928
Etching: sheet, 10¾ x 7¼ (27.3 x 18.4); image, 6 x 4 (15.2 x 10.2)
Bequest of Felicia Meyer Marsh 80.31.119

Conversation, 1931
Etching: sheet, 11¼ x 9½ (28.6 x 24.1); image, 5¹⁵⁄₁₆ x 4 (15.1 x 10.2)
Bequest of Felicia Meyer Marsh 80.31.142*

On the Street (Fourteenth Street), 1931
Etching: sheet, 7⅛ x 14⅛ (18.1 x 35.9);
image, 4⅞ x 10¾ (12.4 x 27.3)
Bequest of Felicia Meyer Marsh 80.31.121

Reading the Newspaper (Two Men Standing) (Two Men), 1931
Etching: sheet, 10¾ x 7¼ (27.3 x 18.4);
image, $6^{15}/_{16}$ x $4^{15}/_{16}$ (17.6 x 12.6)
Bequest of Felicia Meyer Marsh 80.31.145*

Noon Hour, 1935
Etching: sheet, 9⅞ x 8 (25.1 x 20.3);
image, $6^{15}/_{16}$ x $4^{13}/_{16}$ (17.6 x 12.2)
Gift of Mr. and Mrs. Sylvan Cole, Jr. 79.71*

Showing the Snapshot, from the portfolio *Eight Etchings 1936–1959*, 1936
Etching: sheet, 13 x 10 (33 x 25.4);
image, 4 x 3 (10.2 x 7.6)
Gift of the artist and Associated American Artists 81.20.1

Office Girls, from the portfolio *Eight Etchings 1938–1959*, 1938
Etching: sheet, 12⅞ x 9⅞ (32.7 x 25.1);
image, 7⅞ x 4⅞ (20 x 12.4)
Gift of the artist and Associated American Artists 78.43.1*

Office Girls, 1938
Etching: sheet, 11⅛ x 7⅝ (28.2 x 19.3);
image, 8 x 5 (20.3 x 12.7)
Bequest of Felicia Meyer Marsh 80.31.144

Lunch Counter, from the portfolio *Eight Etchings 1938–1959*, 1940
Etching: sheet, 12⅞ x 9⅞ (32.7 x 25.1);
image, 7⅜ x 3⅞ (18.7 x 9.8)
Gift of the artist and Associated American Artists 78.43.2

Lunch Counter, 1940
Etching: sheet, 11 x 7¾ (27.9 x 19.7);
image, 7½ x $3^{15}/_{16}$ (19 x 10)
Bequest of Felicia Meyer Marsh 80.31.143

Strap Hangers, from the portfolio *Eight Etchings 1938–1959*, 1940
Etching: sheet, 12⅞ x 9⅞ (32.7 x 25.1);
image, 6⅞ x 4 (17.5 x 10.2)
Gift of the artist and Associated American Artists 78.43.3

Encounter, from the portfolio *Eight Etchings 1938–1959*, 1941
Etching: sheet, 12⅞ x 9⅞ (32.7 x 25.1);
image, 8⅛ x $5^{7}/_{16}$ (20.6 x 13.8)
Gift of the artist and Associated American Artists 78.43.4*

Reaching for the Coat Sleeve, from the portfolio *Eight Etchings 1936–1959*, 1943
Etching: sheet, 13 x 10 (33 x 25.4);
image, 5⅞ x 4 (15 x 10.2)
Gift of the artist and Associated American Artists 81.20.2

Girl with Newspaper, from the portfolio *Eight Etchings 1936–1959*, 1945
Etching: sheet, 13 x 10 (33 x 25.4);
image, 7⅜ x 4⅜ (18.7 x 11.2)
Gift of the artist and Associated American Artists 81.20.3

Ice Cream Cones #1, from the portfolio *Eight Etchings 1938–1959*, 1945
Etching: sheet, 12⅞ x 9⅞ (32.7 x 25.1);
image, 7⅜ x 4 (18.7 x 10.2)
Gift of the artist and Associated American Artists 78.43.5

Double Date Delayed (Entry—E), from the portfolio *Eight Etchings 1938–1959*, 1948
Etching: sheet, 12⅞ x 9⅞ (32.7 x 25.1); image, 5 x 3 7/16 (12.7 x 8.7)
Gift of the artist and Associated American Artists 78.43.6

Double Date Delayed (Entry—E), 1948
Etching: sheet, 10 x 6¾ (25.4 x 17.2); image, 5 x 3½ (12.7 x 8.9)
Bequest of Felicia Meyer Marsh 80.31.117

Seated Woman with Hat, from the portfolio *Eight Etchings 1936–1959*, 1949
Etching: sheet, 13 x 10 (33 x 25.4); image, 5⅞ x 4 (15 x 10.2)
Gift of the artist and Associated American Artists 81.20.4

Fourteenth Street Oriental, from the portfolio *Eight Etchings 1936–1959*, 1950
Etching: sheet, 13 x 10 (33 x 25.4); image, 5⅞ x 4 (15 x 10.2)
Gift of the artist and Associated American Artists 81.20.5

Fourteenth Street Oriental, 1950
Etching: sheet, 11½ x 8 (29.2 x 20.3); image, 6 x 4 (15.2 x 10.2)
Bequest of Felicia Meyer Marsh 80.31.118

Strap Hangers No. 2, from the portfolio *Eight Etchings 1936–1959*, 1950
Etching: sheet, 13 x 10 (33 x 25.4); image, 4⅞ x 3 (12.5 x 7.7)
Gift of the artist and Associated American Artists 81.20.6

Outdoor Soda Fountain, from the portfolio *Eight Etchings 1938–1959*, 1953
Etching: sheet, 12⅞ x 9⅞ (32.7 x 25.1); image, 6¼ x 4 3/16 (15.9 x 10.6)
Gift of the artist and Associated American Artists 78.43.7

Outdoor Soda Fountain, 1953
Etching: sheet, 9½ x 6⅜ (24.1 x 16.2); image, 6¼ x 4 3/16 (15.9 x 10.6)
Bequest of Felicia Meyer Marsh 80.31.147*

Two Girls Outdoors (Helping with the Veil), from the portfolio *Eight Etchings 1936–1959*, 1953
Etching: sheet, 13 x 10 (33 x 25.4); image, 7½ x 4⅞ (19 x 12.4)
Gift of the artist and Associated American Artists 81.20.7

Girl Getting on Soda Fountain Stool, from the portfolio *Eight Etchings 1936–1959*, 1959
Etching: sheet, 13 x 10 (33 x 25.4); image, 5⅜ x 4 (13.7 x 10.2)
Gift of the artist and Associated American Artists 81.20.8

Snack Bar, from the portfolio *Eight Etchings 1938–1959*, 1959
Etching: sheet, 12⅞ x 9⅞ (32.7 x 25.1); image, 6 13/16 x 4½ (17.3 x 11.4)
Gift of the artist and Associated American Artists 78.43.8

Ilya Bolotowsky (1907–1981)

Untitled, from the portfolio *American Abstract Artists*, 1937
Offset lithograph: sheet and image, 9¼ x 12 (23.5 x 30.5)
Gift of Mr. and Mrs. Wolf Kahn in honor of Alice Mason 77.121.2

Richard Bosman (b. 1944)

Survivor, 1982–83
Woodcut: sheet, 38¼ x 25¾ (97.2 x 65.4); image, 38 x 23⅞ (96.5 x 60.6)
Purchase, with funds from the Print Purchase Fund 83.52*

Harry Bowden (1907–1965)

Untitled, from the portfolio *American Abstract Artists*, c. 1937
Offset lithograph: sheet, 12 x 9 ¼ (30.5 x 23.5); image, 11 ⅛ x 6 ¼ (28.3 x 15.9)
Gift of Mr. and Mrs. Wolf Kahn in honor of Alice Mason 77.121.3

Byron Browne (1907–1961)

Untitled, from the portfolio *American Abstract Artists*, 1937
Offset lithograph: sheet, 12 x 9 ¼ (30.5 x 23.5); image, 9 ½ x 6 ½ (24.1 x 16.5)
Gift of Mr. and Mrs. Wolf Kahn in honor of Alice Mason 77.121.4

Charles Burchfield (1893–1967)

Summer Benediction, 1951–52
Lithograph: sheet, 15 ⅞ x 11 ½ (40.3 x 29.2); image, 12 x 9 ⅛ (30.5 x 23.2)
Gift of Dr. and Mrs. David B. Pall 74.24*

Andrew Butler (b. 1896)

The Siding, 1930
Etching: sheet, 11 11/16 x 15 ½ (29.7 x 39.4); image, 6 15/16 x 8 15/16 (17.6 x 22.7)
Gift of Mr. and Mrs. Michael H. Irving 78.81

Paul Cadmus (b. 1904)

Shore Leave, 1935
Etching: sheet, 13 ⅜ x 15 ¾ (34 x 40); image, 10 7/16 x 11 9/16 (26.5 x 29.4)
Bequest of Felicia Meyer Marsh 80.31.146*

John Cage (b. 1912)

30 Drawings by Thoreau, from *A Portfolio of Seven Prints Recording Collaborations with the Merce Cunningham Dance Company*, Artist's Proof, 1974
Screenprint: sheet and image, 30 x 20 (76.2 x 50.8)
Gift of Calvin Tomkins 80.34.1

John Cage with Calvin Sumsion (b. ?)

Lithograph A, from the portfolio *Not Wanting to Say Anything About Marcel*, 1969
Lithograph: sheet and image, 27 ⅝ x 40 ¼ (70.2 x 102.2)
Gift of Mr. and Mrs. Sylvan Cole, Jr. 81.35.3

Alexander Calder (1898–1976)

The Big I, 1944
Etching and soft-ground etching: sheet, 11 7/16 x 16 5/16 (29.1 x 41.4); image, 6 ⅞ x 8 ⅞ (17.5 x 22.5)
Purchase, with funds from the Print Committee 83.47

Portrait of Yves Elléouët, from *La Proue de la table*, 1967
Etching: sheet, 11 ¼ x 14 ⅞ (28.6 x 37.8); image, 6 ½ x 9 ¼ (16.5 x 23.5)
Gift of Dr. and Mrs. David B. Pall in honor of John I. H. Baur 74.78

The Red Nose, 1969
Lithograph: sheet and image, 29 ½ x 43 ⅜ (74.9 x 110.2)
Promised gift of Howard and Jean Lipman P.39.80

Fêtes, 1971
Book of seven embossed etchings, with text by Jacques Prévert: each sheet, 17¾ x 26¼ (45.1 x 66.7)
Gift of the Howard and Jean Lipman Foundation, Inc. 74.123.1–7

Contour Plowing, 1976
Lithograph: sheet and image, 26⅜ x 38⅛ (67 x 96.8)
Purchase 75.31

Flying Colors '76, 1976
Lithograph: sheet and image, 25 x 35½ (63.5 x 90.2)
Gift of the Employees of Braniff Airways, Inc. 76.20

The Horse, 1976
Lithograph: sheet and image, 29⅝ x 21¼ (75.3 x 54)
Gift of Brewster Fine Arts Ltd. 77.90

JOHN CARROLL (1892–1959)

Yasuo Kuniyoshi and His Friends, 1925
Lithograph with chine collé: sheet, 12¾ x 18½ (32.4 x 47); image, 9⅝ x 10⅞ (24.4 x 27.6)
Purchase, with funds from the Print Purchase Fund 77.86*

FEDERICO CASTELLON (1914–1971)

The Gordian Knot, 1936
Lithograph: sheet, 12⅞ x 17⅞ (32.7 x 45.4); image, 8⅞ x 14 (22.5 x 35.6)
Gift of Mr. and Mrs. Benjamin Weiss 79.66.22

Landscape in Spain, 1937
Lithograph: sheet, 12⅜ x 17⅞ (31.4 x 45.4); image, 9 13/16 x 13¾ (24.9 x 34.9)
Gift of Mr. and Mrs. Benjamin Weiss 79.66.26

Of Land and Sea, 1939
Lithograph: sheet, 16⅛ x 12 (41 x 30.5); image, 10 7/16 x 9 15/16 (26.5 x 25.2)
Gift of Mr. and Mrs. Benjamin Weiss 79.66.25*

Ex Librus, c. 1940
Etching and aquatint: sheet, 10¼ x 7¾ (26 x 19.7); image, 6 x 3⅞ (15.2 x 9.8)
Gift of Mr. and Mrs. Benjamin Weiss 79.66.5

Memories, c. 1940
Lithograph: sheet, 19¼ x 12⅝ (48.9 x 32.1); image, 12⅝ x 9 7/16 (32.1 x 24)
Gift of Mr. and Mrs. Benjamin Weiss 79.66.9*

Study (Figure), c. 1940
Etching: sheet, 8⅛ x 6 1/16 (20.6 x 15.4); image, 6 x 4 (15.2 x 10.2)
Gift of Mr. and Mrs. Benjamin Weiss 79.66.66

Adam and Eve (Nude Couple and Dressed Girl), 1941
Etching: sheet, 10¼ x 7⅝ (26 x 19.4); image, 5 x 3 15/16 (12.7 x 10)
Gift of Mr. and Mrs. Benjamin Weiss 79.66.28

Road in Arizona, c. 1941
Lithograph: sheet, 12⅝ x 19 (32.1 x 48.3); image, 9⅞ x 13⅝ (25.1 x 34.6)
Gift of Mr. and Mrs. Benjamin Weiss 79.66.29

Two Nudes, c. 1941
Etching: sheet, 8⅛ x 11⅛ (20.6 x 28.2); image, 4 x 5⅞ (10.2 x 14.9)
Gift of Mr. and Mrs. Benjamin Weiss 79.66.39

The Aging Graces, 1942
Etching: sheet, 7½ x 10¼ (19 x 26); image, 5⅞ x 8 (14.9 x 20.3)
Gift of Mr. and Mrs. Benjamin Weiss 79.66.38

The Argument, c. 1942
Etching: sheet, 10⅜ x 7⅝ (26.4 x 19.4); image, 7 15/16 x 5⅞ (20.2 x 14.9)
Gift of Mr. and Mrs. Benjamin Weiss 79.66.15

Artist and Model (Double Portrait), 1942
Etching and aquatint: sheet, 9 3/8 x 7 1/2 (23.8 x 19); image, 5 x 3 1/2 (12.7 x 8.9)
Gift of Mr. and Mrs. Benjamin Weiss 79.66.30

The Elder (The Abandoned Patriarch), 1942
Etching: sheet, 7 1/2 x 9 7/16 (19 x 24); image, 4 7/8 x 7 (12.4 x 17.8)
Gift of Mr. and Mrs. Benjamin Weiss 79.66.37

Le Mélange chez Mme. X, 1942
Etching: sheet, 10 1/4 x 7 3/4 (26 x 19.7); image, 5 15/16 x 3 7/8 (15.1 x 9.8)
Gift of Mr. and Mrs. Benjamin Weiss 79.66.32

Mexican Couple, U.S.A., 1942
Etching: sheet, 8 x 10 15/16 (20.3 x 27.8); image, 5 15/16 x 7 7/8 (15.1 x 20)
Gift of Mr. and Mrs. Benjamin Weiss 79.66.33

A Mother's Sorrow (Eve's Sorrow), 1942
Etching: sheet, 10 5/16 x 7 11/16 (26.2 x 19.5); image, 7 7/8 x 5 7/8 (20 x 14.9)
Gift of Mr. and Mrs. Benjamin Weiss 79.66.31

The Proposal, c. 1942
Etching: sheet, 10 1/4 x 7 3/4 (26 x 19.7); image, 4 15/16 x 3 7/8 (12.5 x 9.8)
Gift of Mr. and Mrs. Benjamin Weiss 79.66.40

Santa Clara (Acoma Pueblo), 1942
Etching: sheet, 10 3/16 x 7 11/16 (25.9 x 19.5); image, 7 7/8 x 5 7/8 (20 x 14.9)
Gift of Mr. and Mrs. Benjamin Weiss 79.66.34

Self-Portrait with H, 1942
Etching: sheet, 10 1/4 x 7 9/16 (26 x 19.2); image, 7 7/8 x 5 7/8 (20 x 14.9)
Gift of Mr. and Mrs. Benjamin Weiss 79.66.35

Taos Tryst, Trial Proof, c. 1942
Etching: sheet, 13 x 16 7/8 (33 x 42.9); image, 7 3/4 x 11 7/8 (19.7 x 30.2)
Gift of Mr. and Mrs. Benjamin Weiss 79.66.36

Visiting Day, 1942
Etching: sheet, 10 x 7 5/8 (25.4 x 19.4); image, 7 15/16 x 5 7/8 (20.2 x 14.9)
Gift of Mr. and Mrs. Benjamin Weiss 79.66.41

Les Femmes Reston (Les Femmes restantes), c. 1946
Etching: sheet, 7 1/2 x 9 7/16 (19.1 x 24); image, 4 15/16 x 6 15/16 (12.5 x 17.6)
Gift of Mr. and Mrs. Benjamin Weiss 79.66.53

Greek Myth #1 (Prometheus), Trial Proof, 1947
Etching: sheet, 13 1/16 x 9 7/8 (33.2 x 25.1); image, 8 3/4 x 6 11/16 (22.2 x 17)
Gift of Mr. and Mrs. Benjamin Weiss 79.66.51

Indian Ménage, 1947
Etching and aquatint: sheet, 8 15/16 x 11 15/16 (22.7 x 30.3); image, 6 x 7 11/16 (15.2 x 19.5)
Gift of Mr. and Mrs. Benjamin Weiss 79.66.43

The Judgement of Paris, 1947
Etching: sheet, 11 x 7 7/8 (27.9 x 20); image, 4 15/16 x 3 15/16 (12.5 x 10)
Gift of Mr. and Mrs. Benjamin Weiss 79.66.44

Lovers in the Studio (The Studio), 1947
Etching: sheet, 10 15/16 x 8 (27.8 x 20.3); image, 8 x 5 13/16 (20.3 x 14.8)
Gift of Mr. and Mrs. Benjamin Weiss 79.66.47

Noonday Meal, from the *China Portfolio*, 1947
Etching: sheet, 14 7/8 x 12 3/16 (37.8 x 30.9); image, 9 7/8 x 7 3/4 (25.1 x 19.7)
Gift of Mr. and Mrs. Benjamin Weiss 79.66.8

Portrait for Small Trio (Head with Drape), State I, 1947
Etching: sheet, 10 1/2 x 7 5/8 (26.7 x 19.4); image, 5 x 3 15/16 (12.7 x 10)
Gift of Mr. and Mrs. Benjamin Weiss 79.66.45

Trio, 1947
Etching: sheet, 9 3/4 x 7 5/8 (27.8 x 19.7); image, 4 15/16 x 3 7/8 (12.5 x 9.8)
Gift of Mr. and Mrs. Benjamin Weiss 79.66.46

Acteon and Diana (Four Heads), Trial Proof, c. 1948
Etching: sheet, $9\frac{7}{8}$ x $13\frac{1}{16}$ (25.1 x 33.2);
image, $5\frac{1}{2}$ x $9\frac{1}{8}$ (14 x 23.2)
Gift of Mr. and Mrs. Benjamin Weiss 79.66.49

The Byzantine Bathers, 1948
Etching and aquatint: sheet, $13\frac{7}{8}$ x $10\frac{3}{4}$
(35.2 x 27.3); image, 12 x $8\frac{15}{16}$ (30.5 x 22.7)
Gift of Mr. and Mrs. Benjamin Weiss 79.66.16

Conversation in the Dark, c. 1948
Etching: sheet, $10\frac{1}{2}$ x $7\frac{5}{8}$ (26.7 x 19.4);
image, 8 x $5\frac{7}{8}$ (20.3 x 14.9)
Gift of Mr. and Mrs. Benjamin Weiss 79.66.42

Diana and Acteon #1, Trial Proof, 1948
Etching: sheet, $9\frac{13}{16}$ x 13 (24.9 x 33);
image, $5\frac{7}{16}$ x $9\frac{1}{16}$ (13.8 x 23)
Gift of Mr. and Mrs. Benjamin Weiss 79.66.6

The Golden Apples, 1948
Etching and aquatint: sheet, $14\frac{7}{8}$ x $12\frac{1}{2}$
(37.8 x 31.7); image, $9\frac{1}{4}$ x $5\frac{3}{8}$ (23.5 x 13.6)
Gift of Mr. and Mrs. Benjamin Weiss 79.66.10

Leda and the Swan, Trial Proof, 1948
Etching: sheet, $15\frac{13}{16}$ x 12 (40.2 x 30.5);
image, $11\frac{7}{8}$ x $7\frac{3}{4}$ (30.2 x 19.7)
Gift of Mr. and Mrs. Benjamin Weiss 79.66.50

The Misunderstanding, 1948
Etching: sheet, $10\frac{3}{8}$ x $8\frac{3}{16}$ (26.4 x 20.8);
image, $6\frac{15}{16}$ x $4\frac{15}{16}$ (17.6 x 12.5)
Gift of Mr. and Mrs. Benjamin Weiss 79.66.52

The Proposition, 1948
Etching and aquatint: sheet, $9\frac{7}{16}$ x $7\frac{1}{2}$ (24 x 19);
image, 7 x $4\frac{15}{16}$ (17.8 x 12.5)
Gift of Mr. and Mrs. Benjamin Weiss 79.66.48

The Return of the Prodigal, c. 1948
Etching and aquatint: sheet, $13\frac{1}{2}$ x $12\frac{1}{2}$
(34.3 x 31.7); image, $10\frac{7}{8}$ x $9\frac{5}{16}$ (27.6 x 23.7)
Gift of Mr. and Mrs. Benjamin Weiss 79.66.20

La Toilette, Trial Proof, 1948
Etching: sheet, $13\frac{1}{8}$ x $9\frac{7}{8}$ (33.3 x 25.1);
image, $5\frac{3}{16}$ x $5\frac{7}{16}$ (13.2 x 13.8)
Gift of Mr. and Mrs. Benjamin Weiss 79.66.11

Conversation Piece (Words of Wisdom), c. 1949
Etching: sheet, $11\frac{3}{8}$ x $9\frac{1}{8}$ (28.9 x 23.2);
image, 8 x $5\frac{15}{16}$ (20.3 x 15.1)
Gift of Mr. and Mrs. Benjamin Weiss 79.66.17

Melancholia, 1949
Etching and aquatint: sheet, 16 x $11\frac{7}{16}$
(40.6 x 29.1); image, $11\frac{7}{8}$ x $8\frac{15}{16}$ (30.2 x 22.7)
Gift of Mr. and Mrs. Benjamin Weiss 79.66.19

Paris in the House, 1949
Etching: sheet, $7\frac{1}{2}$ x $9\frac{7}{16}$ (19.1 x 24);
image, $4\frac{5}{8}$ x 5 (11.7 x 12.7)
Gift of Mr. and Mrs. Benjamin Weiss 79.66.54

The Brawl, 1950
Etching and aquatint: sheet, 13 x $11\frac{3}{4}$
(33 x 29.8); image, 11 x $9\frac{1}{2}$ (27.9 x 23.5)
Gift of Mr. and Mrs. Benjamin Weiss 79.66.18

Ring Bell, c. 1950
Etching and aquatint: sheet, $11\frac{5}{16}$ x $9\frac{1}{8}$
(28.7 x 23.2); image, 8 x $5\frac{15}{16}$ (20.3 x 15.1)
Gift of Mr. and Mrs. Benjamin Weiss 79.66.21

Woman Threading Needle, c. 1950
Etching and aquatint: sheet, $13\frac{3}{16}$ x $11\frac{15}{16}$
(33.5 x 30.3); image, $10\frac{7}{8}$ x $9\frac{1}{4}$ (27.6 x 23.5)
Gift of Mr. and Mrs. Benjamin Weiss 79.66.55

Two Draped Nudes, c. 1952
Linocut: sheet, $10\frac{3}{4}$ x $7\frac{5}{8}$ (27.3 x 19.4);
image, $7\frac{1}{16}$ x $5\frac{5}{8}$ (17.9 x 14.3)
Gift of Mr. and Mrs. Benjamin Weiss 79.66.13

Mother and Child, c. 1958
Linocut: sheet, 8 x $10\frac{7}{8}$ (20.3 x 27.6);
image, 3 x $5\frac{3}{4}$ (7.6 x 14.6)
Gift of Mr. and Mrs. Benjamin Weiss 79.66.7

Three Nudes, c. 1958
Linocut: sheet, 10¾ x 7½ (27.3 x 19.1);
image, 5 x 3¾ (12.7 x 9.5)
Gift of Mr. and Mrs. Benjamin Weiss 79.66.12

Two Reclining Women and a Seated Man, c. 1958
Linocut: sheet, 11 x 7⅝ (27.9 x 19.4);
image, 7 x 5 (17.8 x 12.7)
Gift of Mr. and Mrs. Benjamin Weiss 79.66.56

Two Seated Figures, c. 1958
Linocut: sheet, 11 x 7⅝ (27.9 x 19.4);
image, 5 x 4½ (12.7 x 11.4)
Gift of Mr. and Mrs. Benjamin Weiss 79.66.14

Tightrope Walker (Walking a Tight Rope on a Starry Night), 1970
Lithograph: sheet, 30 x 22¼ (76.2 x 56.5);
image, 26¼ x 20⅞ (66.7 x 53)
Gift of the Circle Gallery, Ltd. 73.53

Giorgio Cavallon (b. 1904)

Untitled, from the portfolio *American Abstract Artists*, 1937
Offset lithograph: sheet, 12 x 9¼ (30.5 x 23.5);
image, 9⅛ x 6⅞ (23.2 x 17.5)
Gift of Mr. and Mrs. Wolf Kahn in honor of Alice Mason 77.121.5

Louisa Chase (b. 1951)

Chasm, 1983
Woodcut: sheet, 26 x 30⅛ (66 x 76.5);
image, 23⅞ x 28¹⁄₁₆ (60.6 x 71.3)
Gift of Mr. and Mrs. Thomas H. Dittmer 84.25*

A. N. Christie (1891–?)

Untitled, from the portfolio *American Abstract Artists*, 1937
Offset lithograph: sheet, 12 x 9⅛ (30.5 x 23.2);
image, 8 x 6⅝ (20.3 x 16.8)
Gift of Mr. and Mrs. Wolf Kahn in honor of Alice Mason 77.121.6

Chuck Close (b. 1940)

Keith/Four Times, Artist's Proof, 1970
Lithograph: sheet and image, 29⅞ x 79⅝ (75.4 x 202.3)
Gift of Lawrence and Carol Zicklin 80.47

Glenn O. Coleman (1887–1932)

Bonfire, from the series *Lithographs of New York*, 1928
Lithograph: sheet, 15⅞ x 22¾ (40.3 x 57.8);
image, 13⁵⁄₁₆ x 18⁵⁄₁₆ (33.8 x 46.5)
Gift of Mrs. Herbert B. Lazarus 73.90

Minetta Lane, from the series *Lithographs of New York*, 1928
Lithograph: sheet, 13½ x 13⅛ (34.3 x 33.3);
image, 11⅛ x 11 (28.2 x 27.9)
Gift of Mrs. Herbert B. Lazarus 73.80*

Rockport, 1931
Lithograph: sheet, 15¾ x 20½ (40 x 52.1);
image, 12¼ x 14¾ (31.1 x 37.5)
Gift of Mrs. Herbert B. Lazarus 73.91

Warrington Colescott (b. 1921)

History of Printmaking: S. W. Hayter Discovers Viscosity Printing, from the portfolio *History of Printmaking*, 1976
Etching, aquatint, and soft-ground etching:
sheet, 24⅞ x 35¾ (63.2 x 90.8);
image, 21⅞ x 27¾ (55.6 x 70.5)
Gift of Mrs. Albert A. List 77.57

Howard Cook (1901–1980)

Times Square Sector, 1930
Etching: sheet, 13⅞ x 11½ (35.2 x 29.2);
image, 11¹³⁄₁₆ x 9⅞ (30 x 25.1)
Gift of Associated American Artists 77.17*

The West Side, New York, 1931
Etching and aquatint: sheet, 11 1/2 x 15 3/4 (29.2 x 40); image, 6 11/16 x 12 7/16 (17 x 31.6)
Gift of Mr. and Mrs. Michael H. Irving 78.82*

ROBERT COTTINGHAM (b. 1935)

Orph, 1972
Lithograph: sheet, 24 x 34 (61 x 86.4); image, 20 1/8 x 30 (51.1 x 76.2)
Gift of Dr. and Mrs. Samuel Mandel 79.2

JOHN STEUART CURRY (1897–1946)

Danbury Fair, 1930
Lithograph: sheet, 17 1/4 x 12 15/16 (43.8 x 32.9); image, 13 x 9 3/4 (33 x 24.8)
Gift of Mr. and Mrs. Michael H. Irving 78.83

Horses Running Before a Storm, 1930
Lithograph: sheet, 13 7/8 x 17 (35.2 x 43.2); image, 9 1/2 x 13 1/16 (24.1 x 33.2)
Gift of Mr. and Mrs. Michael H. Irving 78.84

STUART DAVIS (1894–1964)

Barber Shop Chord, 1931
Lithograph: sheet, 20 3/16 x 26 (51.3 x 66); image, 14 x 19 (35.6 x 48.3)
Purchase, with funds from Philip Morris Incorporated 77.84*

Composition, 1931
Lithograph: sheet, 22 7/8 x 15 11/16 (58.1 x 39.8); image, 10 x 9 (25.4 x 22.9)
Promised gift of Mrs. Stuart Davis P.88.77

Sixth Avenue El, 1931
Lithograph: sheet, 15 7/8 x 21 1/8 (40.3 x 53.7); image, 11 15/16 x 18 (30.3 x 45.7)
Purchase, with funds from Mr. and Mrs. Samuel M. Kootz 77.74*

Theater on the Beach, 1931
Lithograph: sheet, 15 13/16 x 22 5/8 (40.2 x 57.5); image, 11 x 15 (27.9 x 38.1)
Purchase, with funds from Mr. and Mrs. Samuel M. Kootz 77.75*

Two Figures and El, 1931
Lithograph: sheet, 20 1/8 x 26 (51.1 x 66); image, 11 x 15 (27.9 x 38.1)
Gift of Mr. and Mrs. Michael H. Irving 77.13*

RICHARD DIEBENKORN (b. 1922)

Black Club, 1981
Etching, aquatint, and drypoint: sheet, 30 1/4 x 22 5/8 (76.8 x 57.5); image, 13 1/2 x 9 1/2 (34.3 x 24.1)
Purchase, with funds from the Print Committee 83.10*

Tri-Color, 1981
Etching, aquatint, and drypoint: sheet, 30 1/2 x 22 (77.5 x 55.9); image, 13 1/2 x 9 1/2 (34.3 x 24.1)
Promised gift of Emily Fisher Landau P.24.83*

MARK DI SUVERO (b. 1933)

Jak, Artist's Proof, 1976
Lithograph and screenprint: sheet and image, 41 3/4 x 29 5/8 (106 x 75.2)
Gift of the artist 76.3

WERNER DREWES (b. 1899)

Untitled, from the portfolio *American Abstract Artists*, 1937
Offset lithograph: sheet, 9 1/4 x 11 7/8 (23 x 30.2); image, 6 7/8 x 9 5/8 (17.5 x 24.5)
Gift of Mr. and Mrs. Wolf Kahn in honor of Alice Mason 77.121.7

Hunting the Sea Monster, State I, 1938–77
Woodcut: sheet, 17⅛ x 10½ (43.5 x 26.7); image, 11 x 7⅛ (27.9 x 18.1)
Gift of Martin Diamond 77.77*

MABEL DWIGHT (1876–1955)

The Survivor, Staten Island, 1929
Lithograph: sheet, 11⅜ x 15⅞ (28.9 x 40.3); image, 9¹⁵⁄₁₆ x 13¹¹⁄₁₆ (25.2 x 34.7)
Gift of Mr. and Mrs. Michael H. Irving 78.85

DON EDDY (b. 1944)

Strictly Kosher Meats, 1973
Lithograph: sheet, 26¾ x 22½ (67.9 x 57.2); image, 24⅛ x 20½ (61.3 x 52.1)
Gift of Dr. and Mrs. Samuel Mandel 77.72*

HERZL EMANUEL (b. 1914)

Untitled, from the portfolio *American Abstract Artists*, 1937
Offset lithograph: sheet, 9⅛ x 12 (23.2 x 30.5); image, 5⅞ x 8¾ (14.9 x 22.2)
Gift of Mr. and Mrs. Wolf Kahn in honor of Alice Mason 77.121.8

RICHARD ESTES (b. 1936)

Untitled, 1974–75
Screenprint: sheet, 35½ x 49¼ (90.2 x 125.1); image, 33¼ x 46¾ (84.5 x 118.7)
Gift of Mr. and Mrs. Edwin S. Marks 78.112*

PHILIP EVERGOOD (1901–1973)

Still Life, 1944
Lithograph: sheet, 12⅞ x 18½ (32.7 x 47); image, 11½ x 16¼ (29.2 x 41.3)
Gift of Mr. and Mrs. Benjamin Weiss 79.66.1

LYONEL FEININGER (1871–1956)

Benz 2, 1919
Woodcut: sheet, 14 x 19⅝ (35.6 x 49.8); image, 9⅛ x 11⁷⁄₁₆ (23.2 x 29.1)
Gift of Mr. and Mrs. Sylvan Cole, Jr. 80.55.1*

Windmill, 1919
Woodcut: sheet, 12 x 18½ (30.5 x 47); image, 10 x 12 (25.4 x 30.5)
Gift of Mr. and Mrs. Sylvan Cole, Jr. 80.55.2*

JOHN FERREN (1905–1970)

Sea Forms, 1937
Wood engraving: sheet, 26¹⁄₁₆ x 19¹³⁄₁₆ (66.2 x 50.3); image, 14½ x 14½ (36.8 x 36.8)
Purchase, with funds from the Print Purchase Fund 78.67*

ERIC FISCHL (b. 1948)

Digging Kids, 1982
Soft-ground and lift-ground etching and aquatint: sheet and image, 54 x 38½ (137.2 x 97.8)
Purchase, with funds from the Print Committee 84.11*

LLYN FOULKES (b. 1934)

In Memory of F. G. Hough #1, 1974
Lithograph: sheet, 19⁵⁄₁₆ x 24⅜ (49.1 x 61.9); image, 15 x 19¾ (38.1 x 50.2)
Gift of Paul Leeman 75.24

In Memory of F. G. Hough #2, 1974
Lithograph: sheet, 22⁵⁄₁₆ x 22¼ (56.7 x 56.5); image, 15⅞ x 16 (40.3 x 40.6)
Gift of Paul Leeman 75.25

In Memory of F. G. Hough #3, 1974
Lithograph: sheet, 22³⁄₁₆ x 22⅜ (56.4 x 56.8); image, 19 x 19 (48.3 x 48.3)
Gift of Paul Leeman 75.26

Mary Frank (b. 1933)

Dinosaur, 1980
Monotype: sheet and image, 24 3/4 x 35 1/2 (62.9 x 90.2)
Purchase, with funds from the Print Committee 83.13*

Helen Frankenthaler (b. 1928)

Lot's Wife, Artist's Proof, 1971
Lithograph on three sheets: sheets and image, 130 1/2 x 35 1/2 (331.5 x 90.2)
Purchase, with funds from the Print Purchase Fund 78.52*

Don Freeman (1909–1978)

Automat Aristocrat, Artist's Proof, 1932
Lithograph: sheet, 11 x 13 (27.9 x 33); image, 7 1/4 x 8 5/16 (18.4 x 21.1)
Gift of The Margo Feiden Galleries 74.102*

The First Washington Square Art Show, Artist's Proof, 1932
Lithograph: sheet, 13 x 16 1/16 (33 x 40.8); image, 9 5/8 x 11 7/8 (24.4 x 30.2)
Gift of The Margo Feiden Galleries 74.101*

On the Fly Rail (Above the Stars), Artist's Proof, 1934
Lithograph: sheet, 13 1/4 x 16 (33.7 x 40.6); image, 9 9/16 x 11 7/8 (24.3 x 30.2)
Gift of The Margo Feiden Galleries 74.100*

Robert Fried (1937–1975)

Farsighted, 1974
Screenprint: sheet, 21 3/4 x 29 5/8 (55.2 x 75.2); image, 13 7/8 x 26 3/8 (35.2 x 67)
Purchase 74.104

Fritz Glarner (1899–1972)

Recollection, 1964–68
Book of fourteen lithographs, with text by the artist: each sheet, 14 1/4 x 22 1/2 (36.2 x 57.2)
Purchase, with funds from the Richard and Dorothy Rodgers Fund 77.83.1–14*

Arshile Gorky (1905–1948)

Mannikin, 1931
Lithograph: sheet, 19 x 14 1/8 (48.3 x 35.9); image, 14 3/4 x 11 3/8 (37.5 x 28.9)
Purchase 74.36*

John Graham (1881–1961)

Untitled, 1930
Lithograph with chine collé: sheet, 12 5/8 x 19 5/8 (32.1 x 49.8); image, 8 13/16 x 11 1/16 (22.4 x 28.1)
Gift of an Anonymous Donor 83.41.1*

Dorothea Greenbaum (b. 1893)

Ravaged Leaf, 1969
Etching: sheet, 10 7/8 x 11 3/8 (27.6 x 28.9); image, 7 3/8 x 6 1/4 (18.7 x 15.9)
Katherine Schmidt Shubert Bequest 83.44.10

Balcomb Greene (b. 1904)

Untitled, from the portfolio *American Abstract Artists*, 1937
Offset lithograph: sheet and image, 9 1/4 x 12 (23.5 x 30.5)
Gift of Mr. and Mrs. Wolf Kahn in honor of Alice Mason 77.121.9

Gertrude Greene (1904–1956)

Untitled, from the portfolio *American Abstract Artists*, 1937
Offset lithograph: sheet, 9¼ x 12 (23.5 x 30.5); image, 5 x 9½ (12.7 x 24.1)
Gift of Mr. and Mrs. Wolf Kahn in honor of Alice Mason 77.121.10

Red Grooms (b. 1937)

Guggenheim, Artist's Proof, 1972
Lithograph: sheet and image, 38⁵⁄₁₆ x 26 (97.3 x 66)
Purchase, with funds from Mr. and Mrs. William A. Marsteller 77.10

Philip Guston (1913–1980)

The Street, 1970
Lithograph: sheet, 22⁵⁄₁₆ x 30¹⁄₁₆ (56.7 x 76.4); image, 19⅝ x 26¼ (49.8 x 66.7)
Gift of Mr. and Mrs. Thomas H. Dittmer 84.26*

Rug, 1980
Lithograph: sheet and image, 19⅜ x 28⅞ (49.2 x 73.3)
Gift of Mr. and Mrs. Thomas H. Dittmer 84.27*

Hananiah Harari (b. 1912)

Untitled, from the portfolio *American Abstract Artists*, 1937
Offset lithograph: sheet, 12 x 9¼ (30.5 x 23.5); image, 7⅞ x 5½ (20 x 14)
Gift of Mr. and Mrs. Wolf Kahn in honor of Alice Mason 77.121.11

Childe Hassam (1859–1935)

The Lion Gardiner House, East Hampton, 1920
Etching: sheet, 12 x 15¹⁵⁄₁₆ (30.5 x 40.5); image, 9⅞ x 14¹⁄₁₆ (25.1 x 35.7)
Gift of Herbert Brook 81.19*

Stefan Hirsch (1899–1964)

Snake, 1931
Etching: sheet, 9½ x 11¾ (24.1 x 29.8); image, 4 x 6 (10.2 x 15.2)
Gift of Mr. and Mrs. Michael H. Irving 78.86

Hans Hofmann (1880–1966)

Untitled, 1961
Screenprint: sheet, 13⅝ x 13 (36.6 x 33); image, 10 x 9¾ (25.4 x 24.8)
Gift of Dr. and Mrs. Antonino Castellett 74.88

Carl Holty (1900–1973)

Untitled, 1936
Lithograph: sheet, 9¹⁵⁄₁₆ x 14 (25.2 x 35.6); image, 8³⁄₁₆ x 10¹⁵⁄₁₆ (20.8 x 27.8)
Gift of Martin Diamond and Vaclav Vytlacil 78.64

Untitled, from the portfolio *American Abstract Artists*, 1937
Offset lithograph: sheet, 11¹⁵⁄₁₆ x 9¹⁄₁₆ (30.3 x 23); image, 9⁹⁄₁₆ x 6¹⁄₁₆ (24.3 x 15.4)
Gift of Mr. and Mrs. Wolf Kahn in honor of Alice Mason 77.121.12

Yvonne Jacquette (b. 1934)

East Fifteenth Street, 1974
Lithograph: sheet and image, 17½ x 21 (44.5 x 53.3)
Gift of Mr. and Mrs. Philip Pearlstein 74.128

Jasper Johns (b. 1930)

Targets, 1967–68
Lithograph: sheet and image, 34 x 25½ (86.4 x 64.8)
Gift of Dr. and Mrs. Harley Shands 77.103

Souvenir, 1970
Lithograph: sheet and image, 30⅝ x 22⅜ (77.8 x 56.8)
Gift of Mr. and Mrs. Stanley L. Helfgott 74.124*

M.D., from *A Portfolio of Seven Prints Recording Collaborations with the Merce Cunningham Dance Company*, Artist's Proof, 1974
Die-cut stencil: sheet and image, 22 x 18 (55.9 x 45.7)
Gift of Calvin Tomkins 80.34.2

Savarin Can with Brushes, 1977
Lithograph: sheet and image, 53½ x 31⅛ (135.9 x 79.1)
Gift of the artist 77.109*

Untitled, 1977
Screenprint: sheet and image, 24 x 19 (61 x 48.3)
Purchase, with funds from the Print Purchase Fund 77.87

Untitled, 1977, cover design for Whitney Museum Jasper Johns exhibition catalogue, 1977
Lithograph: sheet and image, 29½ x 40½ (74.9 x 102.9)
Gift of the artist 77.122*

Savarin, 1977–81
Lithograph: sheet and image, 50 x 38⅛ (127 x 96.8)
Purchase, with funds from the Friends of the Whitney Museum of American Art 82.10*

Savarin, 1978
Monotype: sheet and image, 26 x 19½ (66 x 49.5)
Purchase, with funds from the Print Committee 82.29*

Usuyuki, Artist's Proof, 1979
Lithograph: sheet and image, 34¼ x 50¼ (87 x 127.6)
50th Anniversary Gift of Philip Morris Incorporated 80.19*

Usuyuki, 1979–81
Screenprint: sheet and image, 29⅛ x 46⅞ (74 x 119)
Purchase, with funds from Philip Morris Incorporated 81.34*

Two Flags (Whitney Anniversary, 1980), Artist's Proof, 1980
Lithograph: sheet and image, 50 x 33⅝ (127 x 85.4)
50th Anniversary Gift of the artist 80.10*

Untitled, 1983
Monotype: sheet and image, 32½ x 92½ (82.6 x 234.3)
Purchase, with funds from the Grace Belt Endowed Purchase Fund, the Wilfred P. and Rose J. Cohen Purchase Fund, the Equitable Life Assurance Society of the United States Purchase Fund, S. Sidney Kahn, The List Purchase Fund, Mr. and Mrs. William A. Marsteller, the Print Purchase Fund, and the Print Committee 84.28*

Voice 2, 1983
Offset lithograph: sheet and image, 36½ x 25½ (92.7 x 64.8)
Purchase, with funds from the Print Purchase Fund 83.48*

DONALD JUDD (b. 1928)

Untitled (Diptych), 1961–75
Woodcut: each sheet, 24½ x 33¾ (62.2 x 85.7); images, (a) 15 5/16 x 20 3/16 (38.9 x 51.3), (b) 14⅞ x 20¼ (37.8 x 51.4)
Purchase, with funds from the Print Committee 82.30a–b*

JACOB KAINEN (b. 1909)

Hesperus, 1974
Lithograph: sheet, 24 x 30½ (61 x 77.5); image, 22⅛ x 28⅛ (56.2 x 71.4)
Gift of the artist 74.105

RAY KAISER (b. ?)

Untitled, from the portfolio *American Abstract Artists*, 1937
Offset lithograph: sheet, 12 x 9¼ (30.5 x 23.5); image, 9 x 6¾ (22.9 x 17.1)
Gift of Mr. and Mrs. Wolf Kahn in honor of Alice Mason 77.121.13

ALEX KATZ (b. 1927)

Large Head of Ada, 1972–73
Etching and aquatint: sheet and image, 15 x 40 (38.1 x 101.6)
Gift of Paul J. Schupf in honor of John I. H. Baur 74.35*

Provincetown, Late Afternoon I, 1973
Screenprint: sheet and image, 18 x 24 (45.7 x 61)
Gift of Brooke Alexander 74.41

Vincent with Open Mouth, 1974
Aquatint and drypoint: sheet and image, 14¾ x 22⅛ (37.5 x 56.2)
Gift of Brooke Alexander, Marlborough Graphics, and the artist 74.89*

Face of the Poet, 1978
Book of fourteen aquatints, with poems by Ted Berrigan, Kenward Elmslie, John Godfrey, Ted Greenwald, Michael Lally, Ann Lauterbach, Gerard Malanga, Alice Notley, John Perreault, Carter Ratcliff, Rene Ricard, Peter Schjeldahl, Tony Towle, Bill Zavatsky: each sheet, 14½ x 19 (36.8 x 48.3)
Purchase 79.33.1–14*

ELLSWORTH KELLY (b. 1923)

Wall, 1979
Etching and aquatint: sheet, 31⅝ x 28 (80.4 x 71.1); image, 16¼ x 14 (41.3 x 35.6)
Purchase, with funds from the Print Purchase Fund 79.73*

PAUL KELPE (b. 1902)

Untitled, from the portfolio *American Abstract Artists*, 1937
Offset lithograph: sheet and image, 12 x 9¼ (30.5 x 23.5)
Gift of Mr. and Mrs. Wolf Kahn in honor of Alice Mason 77.121.14

M. KENNEDY (?–?)

Untitled, from the portfolio *American Abstract Artists*, 1937
Offset lithograph: sheet, 9¼ x 12 (23.5 x 30.5); image, 7 x 9¼ (17.8 x 23.5)
Gift of Mr. and Mrs. Wolf Kahn in honor of Alice Mason 77.121.15

ROBERT KIPNISS (b. 1931)

Dark Trees, 1973
Lithograph: sheet, 19½ x 22 (49.5 x 55.9); image, 13$^{15}/_{16}$ x 16$^{15}/_{16}$ (35.4 x 43)
Gift of Dr. and Mrs. Paul Beck 73.67

Hilltop, 1973
Lithograph: sheet, 21$^{13}/_{16}$ x 22½ (53.8 x 57.2); image, 15⅞ x 16$^{15}/_{16}$ (40.3 x 43)
Gift of Dr. and Mrs. Paul Beck 73.68

LEE KRASNER (1908–1984)

The Civet, 1962
Lithograph: sheet and image, 22 x 29$^{15}/_{16}$ (55.9 x 76)
Gift of Pierre LeVai 74.125*

YASUO KUNIYOSHI (1893–1953)

Milking the Cow, 1922
Lithograph: sheet, 11½ x 15⅞ (29.2 x 40.3); image, 8⅝ x 10¼ (21.9 x 26)
Katherine Schmidt Shubert Bequest 83.44.3

Bather on a Rock (Island of Happiness), 1924
Lithograph: sheet, 16 x 11 15/16 (40.6 x 28.7); image, 10 5/8 x 7 3/4 (27 x 19.7)
Katherine Schmidt Shubert Bequest 83.44.2

Fruit in White Bowl (Bowl of Fruit), 1927
Lithograph: sheet, 16 x 22 5/8 (40.6 x 57.5); image, 13 7/8 x 16 1/4 (35.3 x 41.3)
Katherine Schmidt Shubert Bequest 81.43.1*

New England Landscape, 1927
Lithograph: sheet, 11 5/8 x 16 1/8 (29.5 x 41); image, 8 7/8 x 11 5/8 (22.5 x 29.5)
Katherine Schmidt Shubert Bequest 83.44.4

Pears, Grapes and Peaches, 1927
Lithograph: sheet, 23 x 15 7/8 (58.4 x 40.3); image, 16 x 12 3/4 (40.6 x 32.4)
Katherine Schmidt Shubert Bequest 81.43.2

Squash, 1927
Lithograph: sheet, 16 x 11 1/4 (40.6 x 28.6); image, 9 x 10 (22.9 x 25.4)
Katherine Schmidt Shubert Bequest 81.43.3

Three Dancers, 1927
Lithograph: sheet, 15 7/8 x 11 1/2 (40.3 x 29.2); image, 12 x 10 1/4 (30.5 x 26)
Katherine Schmidt Shubert Bequest 83.44.1

The Acrobat, 1928
Lithograph with chine collé: sheet, 18 7/8 x 12 5/8 (47.9 x 32.1); image, 12 1/8 x 9 (30.8 x 22.9)
Katherine Schmidt Shubert Bequest 81.43.4

Bullfight, 1928
Lithograph with chine collé: sheet, 12 5/8 x 16 5/8 (32.1 x 42.2); image, 9 x 9 1/4 (22.9 x 23.5)
Bequest of Felicia Meyer Marsh 80.31.123

Bullfight, 1928
Lithograph with chine collé: sheet, 12 5/8 x 16 5/8 (32.1 x 42.2); image, 9 x 9 1/4 (22.9 x 23.5)
Katherine Schmidt Shubert Bequest 81.43.5

Dancing, 1928
Lithograph with chine collé: sheet, 19 5/8 x 12 3/4 (49.8 x 32.4); image, 11 9/16 x 10 1/4 (29.3 x 26)
Katherine Schmidt Shubert Bequest 81.43.6

Dressing, 1928
Lithograph with chine collé: sheet, 19 5/8 x 12 3/4 (49.8 x 32.4); image, 12 1/2 x 8 9/16 (31.7 x 21.7)
Katherine Schmidt Shubert Bequest 81.43.7

Four Nudes (Café on Blvd. Clichy), 1928
Lithograph with chine collé: sheet, 12 11/16 x 19 11/16 (32.2 x 50); image, 9 3/8 x 13 1/4 (23.8 x 33.7)
Katherine Schmidt Shubert Bequest 81.43.8*

Girl at Table (At the Café), 1928
Lithograph with chine collé: sheet, 18 7/8 x 12 3/4 (48 x 32.4); image, 11 x 8 (27.9 x 20.3)
Katherine Schmidt Shubert Bequest 81.43.9

Girl in Feathered Hat (The Feathered Hat), 1928
Lithograph with chine collé: sheet, 19 11/16 x 12 3/4 (50 x 32.4); image, 7 1/2 x 5 7/8 (19.1 x 14.9)
Katherine Schmidt Shubert Bequest 83.44.5

Girl Putting on a Chemise, 1928
Lithograph with chine collé: sheet, 19 9/16 x 12 3/4 (49.7 x 32.4); image, 8 3/8 x 5 3/8 (21.3 x 13.7)
Katherine Schmidt Shubert Bequest 83.44.6

Girl with Cigarette, 1928
Lithograph with chine collé: sheet, 12 3/4 x 19 11/16 (32.4 x 50); image, 8 1/8 x 11 1/4 (20.6 x 28.6)
Katherine Schmidt Shubert Bequest 83.44.7

Interior with Dress Form, 1928
Lithograph with chine collé: sheet, 19 11/16 x 12 5/8 (50 x 32.1); image, 12 1/2 x 8 1/2 (31.7 x 21.6)
Katherine Schmidt Shubert Bequest 81.43.10

Night Police, Paris, 1928
Lithograph with chine collé: sheet, 12 11/16 x 15 5/8 (32.2 x 39.7); image, 8 1/2 x 10 3/4 (21.6 x 27.3)
Katherine Schmidt Shubert Bequest 81.43.11

Nude at Door, 1928
Lithograph with chine collé: sheet, $19\frac{11}{16}$ x $12\frac{3}{4}$ (50 x 32.4); image, $13\frac{1}{8}$ x $7\frac{3}{8}$ (33.3 x 18.7)
Katherine Schmidt Shubert Bequest 81.43.12

Peaches and Grapes, 1928
Lithograph with chine collé: sheet, $12\frac{11}{16}$ x $19\frac{5}{8}$ (32.2 x 49.8); image, $9\frac{1}{4}$ x $12\frac{15}{16}$ (23.5 x 32.9)
Katherine Schmidt Shubert Bequest 83.44.8

Railroad, 1928
Lithograph with chine collé: sheet, $19\frac{11}{16}$ x $12\frac{3}{4}$ (50 x 32.4); image, $10\frac{3}{8}$ x $9\frac{1}{8}$ (26.4 x 23.2)
Katherine Schmidt Shubert Bequest 81.43.13

Still Life at Window, 1928
Lithograph with chine collé: sheet, $19\frac{11}{16}$ x $12\frac{11}{16}$ (50 x 32.2); image, $12\frac{1}{8}$ x $8\frac{7}{8}$ (30.8 x 22.5)
Katherine Schmidt Shubert Bequest 81.43.14

Wire Walker, 1928
Lithograph with chine collé: sheet, $12\frac{3}{4}$ x $19\frac{5}{8}$ (32.4 x 49.9); image, $7\frac{3}{8}$ x $9\frac{1}{8}$ (18.7 x 23.2)
Katherine Schmidt Shubert Bequest 81.43.15

Circus Performer Balanced on a Ball (Circus Ball Rider), 1930
Lithograph: sheet, $15\frac{13}{16}$ x $11\frac{3}{8}$ (40.2 x 28.9); image, $14\frac{1}{8}$ x $10\frac{1}{4}$ (35.9 x 26.1)
Katherine Schmidt Shubert Bequest 81.43.16

Before the Act, 1932
Lithograph: sheet, $17\frac{1}{2}$ x $12\frac{1}{2}$ (44.4 x 31.8); image, $13\frac{1}{8}$ x $9\frac{1}{2}$ (33.3 x 24.1)
Katherine Schmidt Shubert Bequest 81.43.17

The Shower, 1932
Lithograph with chine collé: sheet, $12\frac{7}{8}$ x $17\frac{1}{2}$ (32.7 x 44.5); image, $9\frac{3}{4}$ x $13\frac{3}{4}$ (24.8 x 34.9)
Katherine Schmidt Shubert Bequest 81.43.27

Artificial Flower, 1934
Lithograph with chine collé: sheet, $21\frac{1}{8}$ x $14\frac{3}{4}$ (53.7 x 37.5); image, $16\frac{1}{4}$ x 10 (41.3 x 25.4)
Katherine Schmidt Shubert Bequest 81.43.18

Artificial Flower, 1934
Lithograph: sheet, $18\frac{1}{4}$ x $12\frac{3}{4}$ (46.4 x 32.4); image, $16\frac{1}{4}$ x 10 (41.3 x 25.4)
Katherine Schmidt Shubert Bequest 83.44.9

Café, 1934
Lithograph with chine collé: sheet, $14\frac{3}{4}$ x $11\frac{1}{2}$ (37.5 x 29.2); image, 10 x $7\frac{7}{8}$ (25.4 x 20)
Katherine Schmidt Shubert Bequest 81.43.19

Dawn, 1934
Lithograph: sheet, $12\frac{1}{2}$ x $18\frac{7}{8}$ (31.7 x 48); image, $9\frac{7}{8}$ x 14 (25.1 x 35.6)
Katherine Schmidt Shubert Bequest 81.43.20

Café No. 2, 1935
Lithograph: sheet, $15\frac{15}{16}$ x $11\frac{1}{2}$ (40.5 x 29.2); image, $12\frac{1}{2}$ x $9\frac{7}{8}$ (31.7 x 25.1)
Katherine Schmidt Shubert Bequest 81.43.21

Taxco, Mexico, 1935
Lithograph: sheet, $22\frac{3}{4}$ x $15\frac{15}{16}$ (57.8 x 40.5); image, 12 x $14\frac{1}{2}$ (30.5 x 36.8)
Katherine Schmidt Shubert Bequest 81.43.26

Western Landscape (Backyard), 1935
Lithograph: sheet, $15\frac{3}{4}$ x $22\frac{3}{4}$ (40 x 57.8); image, $11\frac{1}{8}$ x $14\frac{3}{4}$ (28.3 x 37.5)
Katherine Schmidt Shubert Bequest 81.43.22

Free Lodging, 1938
Lithograph: sheet, $11\frac{7}{8}$ x 16 (30.2 x 40.6); image, $10\frac{1}{4}$ x 15 (26 x 38.1)
Katherine Schmidt Shubert Bequest 81.43.23

Deserted Brickyard, 1939
Lithograph: sheet, 16 x 21 (40.6 x 53.3); image, $10\frac{5}{8}$ x $15\frac{5}{8}$ (27 x 39.7)
Katherine Schmidt Shubert Bequest 81.43.24

New England Landscape (Provincetown Cemetery), 1941
Lithograph: sheet, $11\frac{3}{4}$ x 16 (29.8 x 40.6); image, $9\frac{3}{4}$ x $13\frac{3}{4}$ (24.8 x 34.9)
Katherine Schmidt Shubert Bequest 81.43.25

Armin Landeck (b. 1905)

Manhattan Canyon, 1934
Etching: sheet, 17 3/4 x 10 5/8 (45.1 x 27); image, 14 x 6 13/16 (35.6 x 17.3)
Gift of Mr. and Mrs. William A. Marsteller in memory of Erni Meyer 77.11*

Ibram Lassaw (b. 1913)

Untitled, from the portfolio *American Abstract Artists*, 1937
Offset lithograph: sheet and image, 12 x 9 1/4 (30.5 x 23.5)
Gift of Mr. and Mrs. Wolf Kahn in honor of Alice Mason 77.121.16

Roy Lichtenstein (b. 1923)

Indian with Pony, 1953
Woodcut: sheet, 17 x 10 3/8 (43.2 x 26.3); image, 9 3/8 x 8 7/16 (23.8 x 21.4)
Purchase, with funds from the Print Committee 83.11*

The Reclining Nude, 1980
Woodcut: sheet, 34 7/8 x 40 (88.6 x 101.6); image, 28 1/8 x 33 1/2 (71.4 x 85.1)
Purchase, with funds from the Print Purchase Fund 80.43*

Two Figures with Teepee, 1980
Soft-ground etching, aquatint, and engraving: sheet, 23 1/2 x 20 5/8 (59.7 x 52.4); image, 9 3/4 x 8 11/16 (24.8 x 22.1)
Purchase, with funds from the Neysa McMein Purchase Award 83.27*

Goldfish Bowl, Artist's Proof, 1981
Woodcut: sheet and image, 25 x 18 1/4 (63.5 x 46.4)
Purchase, with funds from the Print Committee 82.31*

Charles Locke (1899–1983)

The Old Street #3, 1931
Lithograph: sheet, 17 1/2 x 11 (44.5 x 27.9); image, 11 1/2 x 8 (29.2 x 20.3)
Gift of Mr. and Mrs. Michael H. Irving 78.87

The Reading Room, 1931
Lithograph: sheet, 17 1/2 x 12 1/4 (44.5 x 31.1); image, 11 1/2 x 8 1/4 (29.2 x 21)
Gift of Mr. and Mrs. Michael H. Irving 78.88

The Thinker, n.d.
Lithograph: sheet, 15 11/16 x 11 1/8 (39.8 x 28.3); image, 10 1/16 x 8 1/8 (25.6 x 20.6)
Katherine Schmidt Shubert Bequest 83.42.11

Robert Longo (b. 1953)

Jules, Gretchen, Mark, 1983
Lithograph with embossing: sheet and image, 36 5/8 x 68 1/8 (93 x 173)
Purchase, with funds from the Print Committee 83.28*

Louis Lozowick (1892–1973)

New York, 1925
Lithograph: sheet, 15 1/16 x 11 3/8 (38.3 x 28.9); image, 10 7/16 x 9 (26.5 x 22.9)
Purchase, with funds from the John I. H. Baur Purchase Fund 77.12*

Coney Island (Luna Park), 1929
Lithograph: sheet, 15 7/8 x 11 7/16 (40.3 x 29.1); image, 12 3/4 x 8 1/2 (32.4 x 21.6)
Purchase, with funds from Lily Auchincloss 78.18*

Subway Construction, 1931
Lithograph: sheet, 11 7/16 x 15 15/16 (29.1 x 40.5); image, 6 5/8 x 13 1/16 (16.8 x 33.2)
Purchase, with funds from Philip Morris Incorporated 77.8*

Helen Lundeberg (b. 1908)

Planets, 1937
Lithograph: sheet, 16 x 12½ (40.6 x 31.7); image, 12 x 9 (30.5 x 22.9)
Purchase, with funds from the M. Anthony Fisher Purchase Fund 81.17*

Agnes Lyall (?–?)

Untitled, from the portfolio *American Abstract Artists*, 1937
Offset lithograph: sheet and image, 12 x 9¼ (30.5 x 23.5)
Gift of Mr. and Mrs. Wolf Kahn in honor of Alice Mason 77.121.17

Sylvia Mangold (b. 1938)

Untitled, 1974
Lithograph: sheet, 29⅝ x 37¼ (75.2 x 94.6); image, 21 15/16 x 30⅛ (55.7 x 76.5)
Purchase 74.49

John Marin (1870–1953)

Brooklyn Bridge, 1911
Etching: sheet, 19¾ x 15 (50.2 x 38.1); image, 11⅜ x 8 15/16 (28.9 x 22.7)
Purchase, with funds from the Print Committee 83.25*

Reginald Marsh (1898–1954)

Merry-Go-Round, 1930
Etching: sheet, 9 x 12¾ (22.9 x 32.4); image, 6¾ x 9¾ (17.1 x 24.8)
Gift of Mr. and Mrs. Michael H. Irving 78.90*

The Barker, 1931
Etching: sheet, 11 x 8¾ (27.9 x 22.2); image, 9¾ x 8 (24.8 x 20.3)
Gift of Mr. and Mrs. Michael H. Irving 78.89*

Bread Line—No One Has Starved, State III, 1932
Etching and engraving: sheet, 9⅞ x 14⅛ (25.1 x 35.9); image, 6⅜ x 11⅞ (16.2 x 30.2)
Katherine Schmidt Shubert Bequest 82.43.1*

Union Square, 1933
Lithograph: sheet, 16 x 11½ (40.6 x 29.2); image, 13½ x 8½ (34.3 x 21.6)
Bequest of Felicia Meyer Marsh 80.31.130

Box at the Metropolitan (They Pay to Be Seen) State II, 1934
Etching and engraving: sheet, 11½ x 9⅜ (29.3 x 23.8); image, 9⅞ x 7⅞ (25.1 x 20)
Katherine Schmidt Shubert Bequest 82.43.2*

N.Y. Skyline, 1936–37
Etching and engraving: sheet, 10½ x 17 9/16 (26.7 x 44.6); image, 5⅞ x 14 15/16 (14.9 x 38)
Katherine Schmidt Shubert Bequest 82.43.3*

Felicia, 1939
Engraving: sheet, 5⅜ x 3¾ (13.2 x 9.5); image, 3⅞ x 2 15/16 (9.9 x 7.5)
Bequest of Felicia Meyer Marsh 80.31.129

Girl Walking in Front of a Brownstone, c. 1950
Lithograph: sheet, 16 x 12 (40.6 x 30.5); image, 13 x 8⅞ (33 x 22.5)
Gift of Mr. and Mrs. Sylvan Cole, Jr. 79.70

Alice Mason (1904–1971)

Untitled, from the portfolio *American Abstract Artists*, 1937
Offset lithograph: sheet and image, 12 x 9¼ (30.5 x 23.5)
Gift of Mr. and Mrs. Wolf Kahn in honor of Alice Mason 77.121.18

JAN MATULKA (1890–1972)

New York Evening, 1925
Lithograph: sheet, 14 7/16 x 19 1/2 (36.7 x 49.5); image, 13 1/4 x 16 (33.7 x 40.6)
Purchase 77.9*

Untitled, c. 1928
Lithograph: sheet, 10 7/8 x 14 5/8 (27.6 x 37.1); image, 10 3/16 x 10 (25.9 x 25.4)
Purchase 78.25*

GEORGE MCNEIL (b. 1908)

Untitled, from the portfolio *American Abstract Artists*, 1937
Offset lithograph: sheet and image, 12 x 9 1/4 (30.5 x 23.5)
Gift of Mr. and Mrs. Wolf Kahn in honor of Alice Mason 77.121.19

Double Head #1, 1974
Lithograph: sheet, 25 x 21 1/2 (63.5 x 54.6); image, 25 x 19 (63.5 x 48.3)
Purchase, with funds from the Print Committee 83.26*

WILLIAM MCNULTY (1884–1963)

Gotham (The Whirlpool), c. 1928
Etching: sheet, 16 x 10 1/2 (40.6 x 26.7); image, 13 1/2 x 7 (34.3 x 17.8)
Gift of Mr. and Mrs. Samuel L. Rosenfeld 78.113

KENNETH HAYES MILLER (1876–1952)

Crouching Nude Beneath a Tree, 1919
Etching: sheet, 10 3/4 x 6 3/4 (27.3 x 17.1); image, 9 x 4 1/2 (22.9 x 11.4)
Gift of Mr. and Mrs. Michael H. Irving 78.91

Figures in Landscape, c. 1921
Etching: sheet, 7 x 6 1/4 (17.8 x 15.9); image, 6 x 4 15/16 (15.2 x 12.5)
Katherine Schmidt Shubert Bequest 82.43.7

Woman Seated on a Rug, c. 1921
Drypoint: sheet, 11 1/2 x 9 (29.2 x 22.9); image, 5 1/2 x 3 1/2 (14 x 9.5)
Purchase 78.116

Man's Head, c. 1923
Etching: sheet, 8 1/2 x 6 3/4 (21.6 x 17.1); image, 6 x 5 (15.2 x 12.7)
Purchase 78.119

Man with Beard, c. 1928
Etching: sheet, 11 1/2 x 7 15/16 (29.2 x 20.2); image, 7 3/4 x 5 3/8 (19.7 x 13.7)
Purchase 78.121

Nurse and Child, c. 1928
Etching: sheet, 11 1/8 x 7 3/4 (28.3 x 19.7); image, 7 x 4 7/8 (17.8 x 12.4)
Purchase 78.125

Leaving the Shop, 1929
Etching: sheet, 11 3/4 x 15 (29.8 x 38.1); image, 7 7/8 x 9 15/16 (20 x 25.2)
Purchase 78.117

Leaving the Shop, 1929
Etching: sheet, 9 1/8 x 11 7/16 (23.2 x 29); image, 7 15/16 x 9 7/8 (20.2 x 25.1)
Purchase 78.118*

Shopper, c. 1929
Etching: sheet, 13 1/4 x 10 3/4 (33.7 x 27.3); image, 8 1/8 x 6 1/2 (20.6 x 16.5)
Purchase 78.123*

Shopper, c. 1929
Etching: sheet, 13 15/16 x 11 5/16 (35.4 x 28.7); image, 8 7/8 x 6 7/8 (22.5 x 17.5)
Purchase 78.124

Shopper with Umbrella, c. 1929
Etching: sheet, 7 15/16 x 5 (18.6 x 12.7);
image, 4 7/8 x 3 15/16 (12.4 x 10)
Purchase 78.130

Shoppers by an Awning (Beside an Awning), 1929
Etching: sheet, 7 3/8 x 6 3/8 (18.7 x 16.2);
image, 6 x 5 (15.2 x 12.7)
Purchase 78.122

Three Shoppers (Three Women), 1929
Etching: sheet, 9 1/2 x 11 3/4 (24.1 x 29.8);
image, 5 1/4 x 6 3/4 (13.3 x 17.1)
Purchase 78.127

Three Shoppers (Three Women), 1929
Etching: sheet, 7 3/4 x 11 (19.7 x 27.9);
image, 5 1/8 x 6 3/4 (13 x 17.1)
Purchase 78.128

Pause by a Window (Waiting for the Bus), 1930
Etching: sheet, 13 1/8 x 6 7/8 (33.3 x 17.5);
image, 9 1/8 x 5 (23.2 x 12.7)
Purchase 78.120

Saleswomen, c. 1930
Etching: sheet, 7 1/2 x 10 1/2 (19.1 x 26.7);
image, 4 7/8 x 5 1/8 (12.4 x 13)
Purchase 78.129

Conversation, c. 1932
Etching: sheet, 6 1/2 x 10 1/8 (16.5 x 25.7);
image, 3 x 4 1/8 (7.6 x 10.5)
Purchase 78.126

(Seated Nude Bather), n.d.
Etching: sheet, 8 1/2 x 11 (21.6 x 27.9);
image, 4 x 5 (10.2 x 12.7)
Bequest of Felicia Meyer Marsh 80.31.136

MALCOLM MORLEY (b. 1931)

Horses, 1969
Screenprint: sheet, 27 1/2 x 30 1/2 (69.9 x 77.5);
image, 23 3/4 x 26 3/4 (60.3 x 67.9)
Gift of Mr. and Mrs. Aldis Browne 74.90

GEORGE L. K. MORRIS (1905–1975)

Untitled, from the portfolio *American Abstract Artists*, 1937
Offset lithograph: sheet, 12 x 9 1/4 (30.5 x 23.5);
image, 11 1/4 x 7 1/2 (28.6 x 19.1)
Gift of Mr. and Mrs. Wolf Kahn in honor of Alice Mason 77.121.20

ROBERT MORRIS (b. 1931)

Untitled, from *A Portfolio of Seven Prints Recording Collaborations with the Merce Cunningham Dance Company*, Artist's Proof, 1974
Screenprint: sheet and image, 22 x 30 (55.9 x 76.2)
Gift of Calvin Tomkins 80.34.3

ROBERT MOTHERWELL (b. 1915)

Celtic Stone, 1971
Lithograph: sheet and image, 41 7/16 x 29 9/16 (105.3 x 75.1)
Purchase 74.34*

Untitled, 1973
Aquatint: sheet, 41 1/2 x 24 1/8 (105.4 x 61.3);
image, 35 x 17 1/4 (88.9 x 43.8)
Gift of the artist in honor of John I. H. Baur 74.66*

Untitled No. 10, 1976
Monotype: sheet and image, 31 x 22 1/4 (78.7 x 56.5)
Gift of an Anonymous Donor 76.38*

El Negro, 1981–83
Book of nineteen offset lithographs, with the poem "El Negro Motherwell" by Raphael Alberti: sheets, 15 x 15 (38.1 x 38.1); 15 x 25 3/4 (38.1 x 65.4); and 15 x 37 3/4 (38.1 x 95.9)
Purchase, with funds from the Library Fellows and the Print Committee 83.32.1–19*

Bruce Nauman (b. 1941)

Caned Dance, from *A Portfolio of Seven Prints Recording Collaborations with the Merce Cunningham Dance Company*, Artist's Proof, 1974
Lithograph: sheet and image, 22 x 30 (55.9 x 76.2)
Gift of Calvin Tomkins 80.34.4

Claes Oldenburg (b. 1929)

Strawberry Bike Seat, 1976
Etching with chine collé and embossing: sheet, 24 3/8 x 18 1/2 (61.9 x 47); image, 7 3/4 x 8 (19.7 x 20.3)
Gift of Mr. and Mrs. Harry Kahn 78.107

Double Screwarch Bridge, State I, 1980
Etching: sheet, 31 1/4 x 57 15/16 (79.4 x 147.1); image, 23 5/8 x 50 5/8 (60 x 128.6)
Purchase, with funds from the Burroughs Wellcome Purchase Fund 82.16*

Double Screwarch Bridge, State II, 1981
Etching and aquatint: sheet, 31 1/8 x 57 7/8 (79.1 x 147); image, 23 5/8 x 50 5/8 (60 x 128.6)
Purchase, with funds from the Felicia Meyer Marsh Purchase Fund 82.17*

Study for *Double Screwarch Bridge*, State II, 1981
Etching with watercolor: sheet, 31 15/16 x 57 1/2 (81.1 x 146); image, 23 5/8 x 50 5/8 (60 x 128.6)
Purchase, with funds from the Wilfred P. and Rose J. Cohen Purchase Fund 82.15*

Double Screwarch Bridge, State II, Working Proof, 1981
Etching and aquatint with graphite and erasure: sheet, 31 1/4 x 57 3/4 (79.4 x 146.7); image, 23 3/4 x 50 3/4 (60.3 x 128.9)
Purchase, with funds from the List Purchase Fund 82.39*

Double Screwarch Bridge, State III, 1981
Etching and aquatint with monotype: sheet, 31 1/4 x 57 13/16 (79.4 x 147.8); image, 23 1/2 x 50 3/4 (59.7 x 128.9)
Purchase, with funds from the Wilfred P. and Rose J. Cohen Purchase Fund 82.40*

Double Screwarch Bridge, State III, Trial Proof, 1981
Etching and aquatint with monotype: sheet, 33 1/8 x 59 13/16 (84.2 x 152.1); image, 23 5/8 x 50 5/8 (60 x 128.6)
Purchase, with funds from the Richard and Dorothy Rodgers Fund 82.18*

Double Screwarch Bridge, State III, Trial Proof, 1981
Etching and aquatint with monotype: sheet, 33 1/8 x 59 3/4 (84.2 x 151.8); image, 23 1/2 x 50 3/4 (59.7 x 128.9)
Purchase, with funds from Philip Morris Incorporated and the Richard and Dorothy Rodgers Fund 82.41*

Double Screwarch Bridge, State III, Trial Proof, 1981
Etching and aquatint with monotype: sheet, 33 3/8 x 59 7/8 (84.8 x 152.1); image, 23 1/2 x 50 3/4 (59.7 x 128.9)
Purchase, with funds from the Wilfred P. and Rose J. Cohen Purchase Fund 82.42*

John Opper (b. 1908)

Untitled, from the portfolio *American Abstract Artists*, 1937
Offset lithograph: sheet and image, 12 x 9 1/4 (30.5 x 23.5)
Gift of Mr. and Mrs. Wolf Kahn in honor of Alice Mason 77.121.21

Alfonso Ossorio (b. 1916)

Janus, Artist's Proof, 1969
Screenprint: sheet, 37 x 27⅞ (94 x 70.8); image, 30¾ x 22½ (78.1 x 57.2)
Gift of the artist 73.55

Fairfield Porter (1907–1975)

Table, 1971
Lithograph: sheet, 32 x 23⅝ (81.3 x 60); image, 28 x 21 (71.1 x 53.3)
Purchase, with funds from the Print Committee 83.29*

Robert Rauschenberg (b. 1925)

Front Roll, 1964
Lithograph: sheet and image, 41 x 25⅝ (104.1 x 65.1)
Purchase, with funds from the Neysa McMein Purchase Award 77.14*

Lawn, 1965
Lithograph: sheet and image, 34⅞ x 26½ (88.6 x 67.3)
Gift of Mr. and Mrs. Stanley L. Helfgott 73.89*

Visitation I, 1965
Lithograph: sheet and image, 30 x 22 (76.2 x 55.9)
Promised gift of Mr. and Mrs. Matthew A. Meyer in honor of John I. H. Baur P.6.74

Cunningham Relief, from *A Portfolio of Seven Prints Recording Collaborations with the Merce Cunningham Dance Company*, Artist's Proof, 1974
Lithograph with embossing: sheet and image, 30 x 22½ (76.2 x 57.2)
Gift of Calvin Tomkins 80.34.5

Glacial Decoy Series (Etching I), 1979
Etching: sheet and image, 24¾ x 16¾ (62.9 x 42.5)
50th Anniversary Gift of John H. Gutfreund in honor of Charles Simon 80.20.1

Glacial Decoy Series (Etching II), 1979
Etching: sheet and image, 24¾ x 16¾ (62.9 x 42.5)
50th Anniversary Gift of John H. Gutfreund in honor of Charles Simon 80.20.2

Glacial Decoy Series (Etching III), 1979
Etching: sheet and image, 24¾ x 16¾ (62.9 x 42.5)
50th Anniversary Gift of John H. Gutfreund in honor of Charles Simon 80.20.3

Glacial Decoy Series (Etching IV), 1979
Etching: sheet and image, 24¾ x 16¾ (62.9 x 42.5)
50th Anniversary Gift of John H. Gutfreund in honor of Charles Simon 80.20.4

Glacial Decoy Series (Etching V), 1979
Etching: sheet and image, 24¾ x 16¾ (62.9 x 42.5)
50th Anniversary Gift of John H. Gutfreund in honor of Charles Simon 80.20.5

Larry Rivers (b. 1923) with Frank O'Hara (1926–1966)

Stones, 1959
Book of twelve lithographs, with poems by Frank O'Hara: each sheet, 18¾ x 24 (47.6 x 61)
Gift of Mr. and Mrs. Joseph L. Braun 77.123.1–12

Arnold Ronnebeck (1885–1947)

Brooklyn Bridge, 1925
Lithograph: sheet, 16 x 11¼ (40.6 x 28.6); image, 12½ x 6½ (31.8 x 16.5)
Gift of Mr. and Mrs. Samuel L. Rosenfeld 78.114*

Wall Street, 1925
Lithograph: sheet, 15¾ x 11¼ (40 x 28.6); image, 12¼ x 6¾ (31.1 x 17.1)
Gift of Mr. and Mrs. Samuel L. Rosenfeld 78.111*

Paramount, 1928
Lithograph: sheet, 15¾ x 11¼ (40 x 28.6); image, 12 x 7¼ (30.5 x 18.4)
Gift of Mr. and Mrs. Samuel L. Rosenfeld 78.115

Jay Rosenblum (b. 1933)

Lyre, 1974
Screenprint: sheet, 26 x 26 (66 x 66); image, 22 x 21¹⁵⁄₁₆ (55.9 x 55.7)
Gift of Herbert S. Adler 74.48

Ralph Rosenborg (b. 1913)

Untitled, from the portfolio *American Abstract Artists*, 1937
Offset lithograph: sheet and image, 9¼ x 12 (23.5 x 30.5)
Gift of Mr. and Mrs. Wolf Kahn in honor of Alice Mason 77.121.22

James Rosenquist (b. 1933)

high pool, 1964–66
Lithograph: sheet and image, 26½ x 40 (67.3 x 101.6)
Gift of Mr. and Mrs. Stanley L. Helfgott 73.88

Susan Rothenberg (b. 1945)

Four Green Lines, 1984
Lithograph: sheet, 30¾ x 35 (78.1 x 88.9); image, 21⅞ x 30 (55.6 x 76.2)
Gift of Mr. and Mrs. Thomas H. Dittmer 84.29*

Ed Ruscha (b. 1937)

Lisp, 1970
Lithograph: sheet and image, 20 x 28 (50.8 x 71.1)
Gift of Judith Harney 79.50

Robert Ryman (b. 1930)

Six Aquatints, 1975, 1975
Portfolio of six aquatints: each sheet and image, approximately 36¼ x 36¼ (92.1 x 92.1)
Gift of Strahl & Pitsch, Inc. 84.36.1–6

Ludwig Sander (1906–1975)

Untitled, 1964
Lithograph: sheet and image, 17¹⁵⁄₁₆ x 22³⁄₁₆ (45.6 x 56.4)
Gift of Mrs. Kay Hillman 78.5

Paul Sarkisian (b. 1928)

Untitled, 1973
Lithograph: sheet and image, 34 x 24 (86.5 x 61)
Gift of Dr. and Mrs. Samuel Mandel 77.73

Louis Schanker (1903–1981)

The Ten Whitney Dissenters, 1935
Woodcut: sheet and image, 17 x 12¼ (43.2 x 31.1)
Gift of the artist 78.78*

Untitled, from the portfolio *American Abstract Artists*, 1937
Offset lithograph: sheet, 12 x 9¼ (30.5 x 23.5); image, 9 x 7 (22.9 x 17.8)
Gift of Mr. and Mrs. Wolf Kahn in honor of Alice Mason 77.121.23

Jai-Alai, 1939
Woodcut: sheet, 12 x 17 (30.5 x 43.2); image, 10¾ x 15 (27.3 x 38.1)
Purchase, with funds from the Print Purchase Fund 78.71*

Jai-Alai, 1939
Woodcut: sheet, 11½ x 15 (29.2 x 35.1); image, 10 x 14 (25.4 x 35.6)
Purchase, with funds from the Print Purchase Fund 78.73*

Football, 1940
Woodcut: sheet, 12 x 15½ (30.5 x 39.4); image, 10 x 13¾ (25.4 x 34.9)
Purchase, with funds from the Print Purchase Fund 78.74*

Football, 1940
Woodcut: sheet, 13 x 18 (33 x 45.7); image, 9¾ x 13¾ (24.8 x 34.9)
Purchase, with funds from the Print Purchase Fund 78.75*

Polo Players, 1940
Woodcut: sheet, 14½ x 16 (36.8 x 40.6); image, 11¾ x 14 (29.8 x 35.6)
Purchase, with funds from the Print Purchase Fund 78.76

JOEL SHAPIRO (b. 1941)

Untitled, 1975
Series of six etchings: each sheet and image, 12½ x 17½ (31.8 x 44.5)
Purchase, with funds from the Print Committee 83.49.1–6*

CHARLES G. SHAW (1892–1974)

Untitled, from the portfolio *American Abstract Artists*, 1937
Offset lithograph: sheet and image, 12 x 9¼ (30.5 x 23.5)
Gift of Mr. and Mrs. Wolf Kahn in honor of Alice Mason 77.121.24

CHARLES SHEELER (1883–1965)

Architectural Cadences, 1954
Screenprint: sheet, 7¾ x 10 (19.7 x 25.4); image, 6¼ x 8¾ (15.9 x 22.2)
Purchase 74.23*

JOHN SLOAN (1871–1951)

The Sidewalk, 1917
Etching: sheet, 9⅝ x 12⅝ (24.4 x 32.1); image, 3⅛ x 6⅜ (7.9 x 16.2)
Katherine Schmidt Shubert Bequest 82.43.4*

Sixth Avenue, Greenwich Village, 1923
Etching: sheet, 9⅜ x 12⅜ (23.8 x 31.4); image, 4⅞ x 6⅞ (12.4 x 17.5)
Katherine Schmidt Shubert Bequest 82.43.5

Long Prone Nude, 1931
Etching and engraving: sheet, 9½ x 16⅞ (24.1 x 42.9); image, 4¼ x 13¾ (10.8 x 34.9)
Katherine Schmidt Shubert Bequest 82.43.6

Nude on the Floor, 1931
Etching: sheet, 7⅝ x 9½ (19.4 x 24.2); image, 4 x 5 (10.2 x 12.7)
Bequest of Felicia Meyer Marsh 80.31.139

Romany Marye in Christopher Street, *1922*, 1936
Etching: sheet, 8 7/16 x 10 7/16 (21.4 x 26.5); image, 6 x 8 (15.2 x 20.3)
Gift of Helen Farr Sloan 80.14*

Snow on the Range, 1937
Etching: sheet, 9⅛ x 16⅞ (23.2 x 42.9); image, 4 x 6 (10.2 x 15.2)
Gift of Helen Farr Sloan 80.15

Sunbathers on the Roof, 1941
Etching: sheet, 8½ x 10½ (21.6 x 26.7); image, 6 x 7 (15.2 x 17.8)
Bequest of Felicia Meyer Marsh 80.31.138*

Esphyr Slobodkina (b. 1908)

Untitled, from the portfolio *American Abstract Artists*, 1937
Offset lithograph: sheet and image, 12 x 9 ¼ (30.5 x 23.5)
Gift of Mr. and Mrs. Wolf Kahn in honor of Alice Mason 77.121.25

David Smith (1906–1965)

Don Quixote, State I, 1952
Lithograph with egg tempera: sheet, 21 ⅞ x 27 ⅞ (55.6 x 70.8); image, 17 ⅞ x 23 13/16 (45.4 x 60.5)
Purchase, with funds from the Print Committee 84.13*

Don Quixote, State II, 1952
Lithograph: sheet, 22 15/16 x 29 ¼ (56.7 x 74.3); image, 17 ⅞ x 23 13/16 (45.4 x 60.5)
Purchase, with funds from the Print Committee 84.12*

T. L. Solien (b. 1949)

Boatman's Rescue, from the portfolio *Fragments of Hope*, 1982
Drypoint with roulette: sheet, 13 ¾ x 17 ⅛ (34.9 x 43.5); image, 7 15/16 x 10 ⅞ (20.2 x 27.6)
Purchase, with funds from the Print Committee 84.10.2*

Handle and Tow, from the portfolio *Fragments of Hope*, 1982
Drypoint with roulette: sheet, 13 ¾ x 17 ⅛ (34.9 x 43.5); image, 7 15/16 x 10 ⅞ (20.2 x 27.6)
Purchase, with funds from the Print Committee 84.10.4*

Memoir Den, from the portfolio *Fragments of Hope*, 1982
Drypoint with roulette: sheet, 13 ¾ x 17 ⅛ (34.9 x 43.5); image, 7 15/16 x 10 ⅞ (20.2 x 27.6)
Purchase, with funds from the Print Committee 84.10.5*

Sunken Treasure, from the portfolio *Fragments of Hope*, 1982
Drypoint with roulette: sheet, 13 ¾ x 17 ⅛ (34.9 x 43.5); image, 7 15/16 x 10 ⅞ (20.2 x 27.6)
Purchase, with funds from the Print Committee 84.10.1*

Tower of Strength, from the portfolio *Fragments of Hope*, 1982
Drypoint with roulette: sheet, 13 ¾ x 17 ⅛ (34.9 x 43.5); image, 7 15/16 x 10 ⅞ (20.2 x 27.6)
Purchase, with funds from the Print Committee 84.10.3*

Raphael Soyer (b. 1899)

Self-Portrait, c. 1920
Lithograph: sheet, 12 x 9 ½ (30.5 x 24.1); image, 8 ¾ x 6 (22.2 x 15.2)
Gift of Mr. and Mrs. Michael H. Irving 78.92*

Sleep, 1931–32
Lithograph: sheet, 15 15/16 x 20 ½ (40.5 x 52); image, 11 ⅛ x 14 (28.3 x 35.6)
Gift of Mr. and Mrs. Benjamin Weiss 79.66.58

Sylvia, 1933–34
Lithograph: sheet, 20 x 16 (50.8 x 40.6); image, 13 ¾ x 9 ½ (34.9 x 24.1)
Gift of Mr. and Mrs. Benjamin Weiss 79.66.59

In the Studio, 1935
Lithograph: sheet, 16 x 11 ½ (40.6 x 29.2); image, 13 ½ x 9 ½ (34.3 x 24.1)
Gift of Mr. and Mrs. Benjamin Weiss 79.66.57

Behind Screen (Model Resting), 1949
Lithograph: sheet, 12 x 9 11/16 (30.5 x 24.6); image, 8 ⅝ x 6 (21.9 x 15.2)
Gift of Mr. and Mrs. Benjamin Weiss 79.66.60

Benton Spruance (1904–1967)

Road from the Shore, 1936
Lithograph: sheet, 13 3/8 x 18 15/16 (34 x 46.5); image, 10 1/8 x 14 3/8 (25.7 x 36.5)
Gift of Mr. and Mrs. Raymond J. Learsy 82.2.5

The People Work—Morning, 1937
Lithograph: sheet, 15 7/8 x 22 3/4 (40.3 x 57.8); image, 13 5/8 x 18 7/8 (34.6 x 48)
Gift of Mr. and Mrs. Raymond J. Learsy 82.2.1*

The People Work—Noon, 1937
Lithograph: sheet, 15 7/8 x 22 3/4 (40.3 x 57.8); image, 13 5/8 x 18 7/8 (34.6 x 48)
Gift of Mr. and Mrs. Raymond J. Learsy 82.2.2*

The People Work—Evening, 1937
Lithograph: sheet, 15 7/8 x 22 3/4 (40.3 x 57.8); image, 13 5/8 x 18 7/8 (34.6 x 48)
Gift of Mr. and Mrs. Raymond J. Learsy 82.2.3*

The People Work—Night, 1937
Lithograph: sheet, 15 7/8 x 22 3/4 (40.3 x 57.8); image, 13 5/8 x 18 7/8 (34.6 x 48)
Gift of Mr. and Mrs. Raymond J. Learsy 82.2.4*

Frank Stella (b. 1936)

York Factory I, 1971
Screenprint and photo-screenprint: sheet, 17 3/8 x 44 1/2 (44.2 x 113); image, 13 3/8 x 40 1/4 (34 x 102.2)
Gift of Mr. and Mrs. Dave H. Williams 82.47.2

Furg, from *A Portfolio of Seven Prints Recording Collaborations with the Merce Cunningham Dance Company*, Artist's Proof, 1974
Screenprint and offset lithograph: sheet and image, 17 x 22 (43.2 x 55.9)
Gift of Calvin Tomkins 80.34.6*

Estoril Five I, 1982
Relief print: sheet and image, 66 x 51 3/8 (167.6 x 130.5)
Promised gift of Judge Steven Robinson P.11.83

Estoril Five II, 1982
Etching and relief print: sheet and image, 66 x 51 3/8 (167.6 x 130.5)
Promised gift of Judge Steven Robinson P.12.83

Estoril Three II, 1982
Etching and relief print: sheet and image, 66 x 51 3/8 (167.6 x 130.5)
Promised gift of Judge Steven Robinson P.10.83

Imola Three I, 1982
Etching and relief print: sheet and image, 66 x 51 3/8 (167.6 x 130.5)
Promised gift of Judge Steven Robinson P.13.83

Pergusa Three, 1982
Etching and relief print: sheet and image, 66 x 51 3/8 (167.6 x 130.5)
Promised gift of Judge Steven Robinson P.14.83

Pergusa Three, State I, 1982
Etching and relief print: sheet and image, 66 x 51 3/8 (167.6 x 130.5)
Promised gift of Judge Steven Robinson P.15.83*

Swan Engraving I, 1982
Etching: sheet and image, 66 x 51 (167.6 x 129.5)
Promised gift of Judge Steven Robinson P.16.83*

Swan Engraving II, 1982
Etching: sheet and image, 66 x 51 (167.6 x 129.5)
Promised gift of Judge Steven Robinson P.17.83*

Swan Engraving III, 1982
Etching: sheet and image, 66 x 51 (167.6 x 129.5)
Promised gift of Judge Steven Robinson P.18.83*

Swan Engraving IV, 1982
Etching: sheet and image, 66 x 51 (167.6 x 129.5)
Promised gift of Judge Steven Robinson P.19.83*

Swan Engraving Square I, 1982
Etching: sheet and image, 53 x 52 (134.6 x 132.1)
Promised gift of Judge Steven Robinson P.20.83

Swan Engraving Square II, 1982
Etching: sheet and image, 53 x 52 (134.6 x 132.1)
Promised gift of Judge Steven Robinson P.21.83

Swan Engraving Square III, 1982
Etching: sheet and image, 53 x 52 (134.6 x 132.1)
Promised gift of Judge Steven Robinson P.22.83

Swan Engraving Square IV, 1982
Etching: sheet and image, 53 x 52 (134.6 x 132.1)
Promised gift of Judge Steven Robinson P.23.83

Talladega Five I, 1982
Relief print: sheet and image, 66 x 51 3/8 (167.6 x 130.5)
Promised gift of Judge Steven Robinson P.9.83*

Talladega Three I, 1982
Etching: sheet and image, 66 x 51 3/8 (167.6 x 130.5)
Promised gift of Judge Steven Robinson P.6.83*

Talladega Three II, 1982
Relief print: sheet and image, 66 x 51 3/8 (167.6 x 130.5)
Promised gift of Judge Steven Robinson P.7.83*

Talladega Three III, 1982
Relief print: sheet and image, 66 x 51 3/8 (167.6 x 130.5)
Promised gift of Judge Steven Robinson P.8.83

HARRY STERNBERG (b. 1904)

Circus #4: "The Rings," 1929
Etching and aquatint: sheet, 11 x 14 (27.9 x 35.6); image, 8 1/4 x 11 3/4 (21 x 29.8)
Gift of Mr. and Mrs. Michael H. Irving 78.94

Principle #3, 1930
Etching and aquatint: sheet, 9 3/4 x 13 3/4 (24.8 x 34.9); image, 8 x 11 1/2 (20.3 x 29.2)
Gift of Mr. and Mrs. Michael H. Irving 78.93

Steel Mills (Bethlehem Steel), 1937
Lithograph: sheet, 15 7/8 x 21 (40.3 x 53.3); image, 10 3/8 x 16 3/8 (26.4 x 41.6)
Gift of Arthur G. Altschul 78.29

JOHN STORRS (1885–1956)

Romantic Evening (Eagle), 1916
Woodcut: sheet, 9 3/4 x 7 7/8 (24.7 x 20); image, 4 x 4 (10.2 x 10.2)
Purchase, with funds from the John I. H. Baur Purchase Fund 82.33*

The Spirit of the Night, c. 1917
Woodcut: sheet, 11 3/8 x 8 1/8 (28.9 x 20.6); image, 6 1/2 x 6 7/16 (16.5 x 16.4)
Gift of the Robert Schoelkopf Gallery Ltd. 80.23*

Beauty and the Beast (Femme nue), State II, 1918
Woodcut: sheet, 10 7/8 x 10 1/4 (27.6 x 27); image, 5 5/16 x 3 1/4 (13.5 x 8.3)
Purchase, with funds from the John I. H. Baur Purchase Fund 82.32*

ALBERT SWINDEN (1899–1961)

Untitled, from the portfolio *American Abstract Artists*, 1937
Offset lithograph: sheet and image, 12 x 9 1/4 (30.5 x 23.5)
Gift of Mr. and Mrs. Wolf Kahn in honor of Alice Mason 77.121.26

WALTER TITTLE (1883–1966)

Edward Hopper, 1918
Etching: sheet, 10 1/2 x 8 (26.7 x 20.3); image, 3 3/4 x 3 1/2 (9.5 x 8.9)
Purchase 79.1

Harold Tovish (b. 1921)

Motion Sequence, c. 1971
Lithograph: sheet, 22 x 30 (55.9 x 76.2); image, 18 x 24 (45.7 x 61)
Gift of an Anonymous Donor in honor of Margaret McKellar 76.19

R. D. Turnbull (b. 1899)

Untitled, from the portfolio *American Abstract Artists*, 1937
Offset lithograph: sheet, 9¼ x 12 (23.5 x 30.5); image, 7¼ x 8½ (18.4 x 21.6)
Gift of Mr. and Mrs. Wolf Kahn in honor of Alice Mason 77.121.27

Richard Tuttle (b. 1941)

In Praise of Economic Determinism, 1973
Lithograph with pencil and punched holes: sheet and image, 31 x 22½ (78.7 x 57.2)
Purchase 74.43

Vaclav Vytlacil (b. 1892)

Untitled, 1934
Lithograph: sheet and image, 9¹⁵⁄₁₆ x 14 (25.2 x 35.6)
Gift of the artist and Martin Diamond 78.65*

Untitled, 1934
Lithograph: sheet, 9¼ x 11¹⁵⁄₁₆ (23.5 x 30.3); image, 6¾ x 8⅞ (17.1 x 22.5)
Gift of the artist and Martin Diamond 78.66*

Untitled, from the portfolio *American Abstract Artists*, 1937
Offset lithograph: sheet, 9¼ x 12 (23.5 x 30.5); image, 6¾ x 9 (17.1 x 22.9)
Gift of Mr. and Mrs. Wolf Kahn in honor of Alice Mason 77.121.28

Andy Warhol (b. 1928)

Electric Chairs, 1971
Portfolio of ten screenprints: each sheet and image, 35⅝ x 48¹⁄₁₆ (90.5 x 122.1)
Gift of Peter M. Brant 73.92.1–10

Electric Chairs, 1971
Portfolio of ten screenprints: each sheet and image, 11⁷⁄₁₆ x 47⅞ (29.1 x 121.6)
Gift of Peter M. Brant 76.54.1–10

Mao Tse-Tung, 1972
Portfolio of ten screenprints: each sheet and image, 36 x 36 (91.4 x 91.4)
Gift of Mr. and Mrs. Peter M. Brant 74.96.1–10*

Vote McGovern-Nixon, 1972
Screenprint: sheet and image, 41½ x 41½ (105.4 x 105.4)
Gift of Fred Mueller 78.98

Flowers, 1974
Portfolio of ten screenprints: each sheet and image, 40½ x 27½ (102.9 x 69.9)
Gift of Peter M. Brant 76.55.1–10

Flowers, 1974
Portfolio of ten screenprints with watercolor: each sheet and image, 40½ x 27½ (102.9 x 69.9)
Gift of Peter M. Brant 76.53.1–10

Merce, from *A Portfolio of Seven Prints Recording Collaborations with the Merce Cunningham Dance Company*, Artist's Proof, 1974
Photo-screenprint: sheet and image, 30 x 20 (76.2 x 50.8)
Gift of Calvin Tomkins 80.34.7*

TOM WESSELMANN (b. 1931)

The Smoker, 1976
Screenprint: sheet and image, 26 x 19½ (66 x 49.5)
Gift of Transworld Art 78.110

H. C. WESTERMANN (1922–1981)

Human Cannonball, 1971
Woodcut: sheet, 18 x 24½ (45.7 x 62.2); image, 16³⁄₁₆ x 20¹⁄₁₆ (41.1 x 51)
Gift of Marion Bolton Stroud 84.22*

FREDERICK J. WHITEMAN (?–?)

Untitled, from the portfolio *American Abstract Artists*, 1937
Offset lithograph: sheet and image, 12 x 9¼ (30.5 x 23.5)
Gift of Mr. and Mrs. Wolf Kahn in honor of Alice Mason 77.121.29

WILLIAM T. WILEY (b. 1937)

Suite of Daze, 1977
Book of fourteen prints, with text by the artist: each sheet, 16¼ x 12½ (41.3 x 31.8)
Purchase, with funds from the Print Committee 83.31.1–14*

Now Here's That Blame Treaty, State II, 1983
Soft-ground etching, aquatint, and drypoint with burnishing: sheet, 51¾ x 41¾ (131.4 x 106.1); image, 44½ x 35½ (113 x 90.2)
Purchase, with funds from the Print Committee 83.30*

TERRY WINTERS (b. 1949)

Morula II, 1983–84
Lithograph: sheet and image, 42⅛ x 32⁷⁄₁₆ (122.2 x 82.4)
Promised gift of Raymond J. Learsy P.3.84*

GRANT WOOD (1892–1942)

In the Spring, 1939
Lithograph: sheet, 11⅞ x 15⅞ (30.2 x 40.3); image, 8¹⁵⁄₁₆ x 11⅞ (22.7 x 30.2)
Gift of Arthur G. Altschul 78.26*

Midnight Alarm, 1939
Lithograph: sheet, 16 x 11¾ (40.6 x 29.8); image, 12 x 7 (30.5 x 17.8)
Gift of Arthur G. Altschul 78.27*

Shrine Quartet, 1939
Lithograph: sheet, 12 x 15⅞ (30.5 x 40.3); image, 7¹⁵⁄₁₆ x 11⅞ (20.2 x 30.2)
Gift of Arthur G. Altschul 78.28*

ADJA YUNKERS (b. 1900)

2nd Dream of the Infanta Isabel II, 1973
Screenprint: sheet, 40⅞ x 27⅞ (103.8 x 70.8); image, 33 x 24 (83.8 x 61)
Gift of Chambord-Darville, Ltd. 73.58

WILFRID M. ZOGBAUM (1915–1965)

Untitled, from the portfolio *American Abstract Artists*, 1937
Offset lithograph: sheet and image, 12 x 9¼ (30.5 x 23.5)
Gift of Mr. and Mrs. Wolf Kahn in honor of Alice Mason 77.121.30